FREE Test Taking Tips DVD Offer

To help us better serve you, we have developed a Test Taking Tips DVD that we would like to give you for FREE. **This DVD covers world-class test taking tips that you can use to be even more successful when you are taking your test.**

All that we ask is that you email us your feedback about your study guide. Please let us know what you thought about it – whether that is good, bad or indifferent.

To get your **FREE Test Taking Tips DVD**, email freedvd@studyguideteam.com with "FREE DVD" in the subject line and the following information in the body of the email:

a. The title of your study guide.

b. Your product rating on a scale of 1-5, with 5 being the highest rating.

c. Your feedback about the study guide. What did you think of it?

d. Your full name and shipping address to send your free DVD.

If you have any questions or concerns, please don't hesitate to contact us at freedvd@studyguideteam.com.

Thanks again!

RICA Test Prep Study Questions

Three RICA Practice Tests for the Reading
Instruction Competence Assessment
[2nd Edition]

TPB Publishing

Interested in buying more than 10 copies of our product? Contact us about bulk discounts:
bulkorders@studyguideteam.com

ISBN 13: 9781628457056
ISBN 10: 1628457058

Table of Contents

Quick Overview

As you draw closer to taking your exam, effective preparation becomes more and more important. Thankfully, you have this study guide to help you get ready. Use this guide to help keep your studying on track and refer to it often.

This study guide contains several key sections that will help you be successful on your exam. The guide contains tips for what you should do the night before and the day of the test. Also included are test-taking tips. Knowing the right information is not always enough. Many well-prepared test takers struggle with exams. These tips will help equip you to accurately read, assess, and answer test questions.

A large part of the guide is devoted to showing you what content to expect on the exam and to helping you better understand that content. In this guide are practice test questions so that you can see how well you have grasped the content. Then, answer explanations are provided so that you can understand why you missed certain questions.

Don't try to cram the night before you take your exam. This is not a wise strategy for a few reasons. First, your retention of the information will be low. Your time would be better used by reviewing information you already know rather than trying to learn a lot of new information. Second, you will likely become stressed as you try to gain a large amount of knowledge in a short amount of time. Third, you will be depriving yourself of sleep. So be sure to go to bed at a reasonable time the night before. Being well-rested helps you focus and remain calm.

Be sure to eat a substantial breakfast the morning of the exam. If you are taking the exam in the afternoon, be sure to have a good lunch as well. Being hungry is distracting and can make it difficult to focus. You have hopefully spent lots of time preparing for the exam. Don't let an empty stomach get in the way of success!

When travelling to the testing center, leave earlier than needed. That way, you have a buffer in case you experience any delays. This will help you remain calm and will keep you from missing your appointment time at the testing center.

Be sure to pace yourself during the exam. Don't try to rush through the exam. There is no need to risk performing poorly on the exam just so you can leave the testing center early. Allow yourself to use all of the allotted time if needed.

Remain positive while taking the exam even if you feel like you are performing poorly. Thinking about the content you should have mastered will not help you perform better on the exam.

Once the exam is complete, take some time to relax. Even if you feel that you need to take the exam again, you will be well served by some down time before you begin studying again. It's often easier to convince yourself to study if you know that it will come with a reward!

Test-Taking Strategies

1. Predicting the Answer

When you feel confident in your preparation for a multiple-choice test, try predicting the answer before reading the answer choices. This is especially useful on questions that test objective factual knowledge. By predicting the answer before reading the available choices, you eliminate the possibility that you will be distracted or led astray by an incorrect answer choice. You will feel more confident in your selection if you read the question, predict the answer, and then find your prediction among the answer choices. After using this strategy, be sure to still read all of the answer choices carefully and completely. If you feel unprepared, you should not attempt to predict the answers. This would be a waste of time and an opportunity for your mind to wander in the wrong direction.

2. Reading the Whole Question

Too often, test takers scan a multiple-choice question, recognize a few familiar words, and immediately jump to the answer choices. Test authors are aware of this common impatience, and they will sometimes prey upon it. For instance, a test author might subtly turn the question into a negative, or he or she might redirect the focus of the question right at the end. The only way to avoid falling into these traps is to read the entirety of the question carefully before reading the answer choices.

3. Looking for Wrong Answers

Long and complicated multiple-choice questions can be intimidating. One way to simplify a difficult multiple-choice question is to eliminate all of the answer choices that are clearly wrong. In most sets of answers, there will be at least one selection that can be dismissed right away. If the test is administered on paper, the test taker could draw a line through it to indicate that it may be ignored; otherwise, the test taker will have to perform this operation mentally or on scratch paper. In either case, once the obviously incorrect answers have been eliminated, the remaining choices may be considered. Sometimes identifying the clearly wrong answers will give the test taker some information about the correct answer. For instance, if one of the remaining answer choices is a direct opposite of one of the eliminated answer choices, it may well be the correct answer. The opposite of obviously wrong is obviously right! Of course, this is not always the case. Some answers are obviously incorrect simply because they are irrelevant to the question being asked. Still, identifying and eliminating some incorrect answer choices is a good way to simplify a multiple-choice question.

4. Don't Overanalyze

Anxious test takers often overanalyze questions. When you are nervous, your brain will often run wild, causing you to make associations and discover clues that don't actually exist. If you feel that this may be a problem for you, do whatever you can to slow down during the test. Try taking a deep breath or counting to ten. As you read and consider the question, restrict yourself to the particular words used by the author. Avoid thought tangents about what the author *really* meant, or what he or she was *trying* to say. The only things that matter on a multiple-choice test are the words that are actually in the question. You must avoid reading too much into a multiple-choice question, or supposing that the writer meant something other than what he or she wrote.

5. No Need for Panic

It is wise to learn as many strategies as possible before taking a multiple-choice test, but it is likely that you will come across a few questions for which you simply don't know the answer. In this situation, avoid panicking. Because most multiple-choice tests include dozens of questions, the relative value of a single wrong answer is small. As much as possible, you should compartmentalize each question on a multiple-choice test. In other words, you should not allow your feelings about one question to affect your success on the others. When you find a question that you either don't understand or don't know how to answer, just take a deep breath and do your best. Read the entire question slowly and carefully. Try rephrasing the question a couple of different ways. Then, read all of the answer choices carefully. After eliminating obviously wrong answers, make a selection and move on to the next question.

6. Confusing Answer Choices

When working on a difficult multiple-choice question, there may be a tendency to focus on the answer choices that are the easiest to understand. Many people, whether consciously or not, gravitate to the answer choices that require the least concentration, knowledge, and memory. This is a mistake. When you come across an answer choice that is confusing, you should give it extra attention. A question might be confusing because you do not know the subject matter to which it refers. If this is the case, don't eliminate the answer before you have affirmatively settled on another. When you come across an answer choice of this type, set it aside as you look at the remaining choices. If you can confidently assert that one of the other choices is correct, you can leave the confusing answer aside. Otherwise, you will need to take a moment to try to better understand the confusing answer choice. Rephrasing is one way to tease out the sense of a confusing answer choice.

7. Your First Instinct

Many people struggle with multiple-choice tests because they overthink the questions. If you have studied sufficiently for the test, you should be prepared to trust your first instinct once you have carefully and completely read the question and all of the answer choices. There is a great deal of research suggesting that the mind can come to the correct conclusion very quickly once it has obtained all of the relevant information. At times, it may seem to you as if your intuition is working faster even than your reasoning mind. This may in fact be true. The knowledge you obtain while studying may be retrieved from your subconscious before you have a chance to work out the associations that support it. Verify your instinct by working out the reasons that it should be trusted.

8. Key Words

Many test takers struggle with multiple-choice questions because they have poor reading comprehension skills. Quickly reading and understanding a multiple-choice question requires a mixture of skill and experience. To help with this, try jotting down a few key words and phrases on a piece of scrap paper. Doing this concentrates the process of reading and forces the mind to weigh the relative importance of the question's parts. In selecting words and phrases to write down, the test taker thinks about the question more deeply and carefully. This is especially true for multiple-choice questions that are preceded by a long prompt.

9. Subtle Negatives

One of the oldest tricks in the multiple-choice test writer's book is to subtly reverse the meaning of a question with a word like *not* or *except*. If you are not paying attention to each word in the question, you can easily be led astray by this trick. For instance, a common question format is, "Which of the following is…?" Obviously, if the question instead is, "Which of the following is not…?," then the answer will be quite different. Even worse, the test makers are aware of the potential for this mistake and will include one answer choice that would be correct if the question were not negated or reversed. A test taker who misses the reversal will find what he or she believes to be a correct answer and will be so confident that he or she will fail to reread the question and discover the original error. The only way to avoid this is to practice a wide variety of multiple-choice questions and to pay close attention to each and every word.

10. Reading Every Answer Choice

It may seem obvious, but you should always read every one of the answer choices! Too many test takers fall into the habit of scanning the question and assuming that they understand the question because they recognize a few key words. From there, they pick the first answer choice that answers the question they believe they have read. Test takers who read all of the answer choices might discover that one of the latter answer choices is actually *more* correct. Moreover, reading all of the answer choices can remind you of facts related to the question that can help you arrive at the correct answer. Sometimes, a misstatement or incorrect detail in one of the latter answer choices will trigger your memory of the subject and will enable you to find the right answer. Failing to read all of the answer choices is like not reading all of the items on a restaurant menu: you might miss out on the perfect choice.

11. Spot the Hedges

One of the keys to success on multiple-choice tests is paying close attention to every word. This is never truer than with words like almost, most, some, and sometimes. These words are called "hedges" because they indicate that a statement is not totally true or not true in every place and time. An absolute statement will contain no hedges, but in many subjects, the answers are not always straightforward or absolute. There are always exceptions to the rules in these subjects. For this reason, you should favor those multiple-choice questions that contain hedging language. The presence of qualifying words indicates that the author is taking special care with his or her words, which is certainly important when composing the right answer. After all, there are many ways to be wrong, but there is only one way to be right! For this reason, it is wise to avoid answers that are absolute when taking a multiple-choice test. An absolute answer is one that says things are either all one way or all another. They often include words like *every*, *always*, *best*, and *never*. If you are taking a multiple-choice test in a subject that doesn't lend itself to absolute answers, be on your guard if you see any of these words.

12. Long Answers

In many subject areas, the answers are not simple. As already mentioned, the right answer often requires hedges. Another common feature of the answers to a complex or subjective question are qualifying clauses, which are groups of words that subtly modify the meaning of the sentence. If the question or answer choice describes a rule to which there are exceptions or the subject matter is complicated, ambiguous, or confusing, the correct answer will require many words in order to be expressed clearly and accurately. In essence, you should not be deterred by answer choices that seem excessively long. Oftentimes, the author of the text will not be able to write the correct answer without

offering some qualifications and modifications. Your job is to read the answer choices thoroughly and completely and to select the one that most accurately and precisely answers the question.

13. Restating to Understand

Sometimes, a question on a multiple-choice test is difficult not because of what it asks but because of how it is written. If this is the case, restate the question or answer choice in different words. This process serves a couple of important purposes. First, it forces you to concentrate on the core of the question. In order to rephrase the question accurately, you have to understand it well. Rephrasing the question will concentrate your mind on the key words and ideas. Second, it will present the information to your mind in a fresh way. This process may trigger your memory and render some useful scrap of information picked up while studying.

14. True Statements

Sometimes an answer choice will be true in itself, but it does not answer the question. This is one of the main reasons why it is essential to read the question carefully and completely before proceeding to the answer choices. Too often, test takers skip ahead to the answer choices and look for true statements. Having found one of these, they are content to select it without reference to the question above. Obviously, this provides an easy way for test makers to play tricks. The savvy test taker will always read the entire question before turning to the answer choices. Then, having settled on a correct answer choice, he or she will refer to the original question and ensure that the selected answer is relevant. The mistake of choosing a correct-but-irrelevant answer choice is especially common on questions related to specific pieces of objective knowledge. A prepared test taker will have a wealth of factual knowledge at his or her disposal, and should not be careless in its application.

15. No Patterns

One of the more dangerous ideas that circulates about multiple-choice tests is that the correct answers tend to fall into patterns. These erroneous ideas range from a belief that B and C are the most common right answers, to the idea that an unprepared test-taker should answer "A-B-A-C-A-D-A-B-A." It cannot be emphasized enough that pattern-seeking of this type is exactly the WRONG way to approach a multiple-choice test. To begin with, it is highly unlikely that the test maker will plot the correct answers according to some predetermined pattern. The questions are scrambled and delivered in a random order. Furthermore, even if the test maker was following a pattern in the assignation of correct answers, there is no reason why the test taker would know which pattern he or she was using. Any attempt to discern a pattern in the answer choices is a waste of time and a distraction from the real work of taking the test. A test taker would be much better served by extra preparation before the test than by reliance on a pattern in the answers.

FREE DVD OFFER

Don't forget that doing well on your exam includes both understanding the test content and understanding how to use what you know to do well on the test. We offer a completely FREE Test Taking Tips DVD that covers world class test taking tips that you can use to be even more successful when you are taking your test.

All that we ask is that you email us your feedback about your study guide. To get your **FREE Test Taking Tips DVD**, email freedvd@studyguideteam.com with "FREE DVD" in the subject line and the following information in the body of the email:

- The title of your study guide.
- Your product rating on a scale of 1-5, with 5 being the highest rating.
- Your feedback about the study guide. What did you think of it?
- Your full name and shipping address to send your free DVD.

Introduction to the RICA

Function of the Test

The Reading Instruction Competence Assessment (RICA) is required for candidates who have been educated in California and are seeking either multiple subject teaching certification for elementary school or the credentials to teach special education (known as an Education Specialist). Candidates for these qualifications must pass the RICA before they are recommended for preliminary credentials. It is not required to pass the RICA to receive certification to teach just one subject. Examinees can range from those attending university programs to those who already have college degrees. Between the years 2008 and 2013, 80% of test takers reported having a bachelor's degree or higher education.

The RICA measures whether a potential candidate has the understanding and proficiencies necessary to teach reading to students. It is one of six teacher certification exams in California that are part of a program called the California Reading Initiative, intended to increase the reading skills and performance of students within the state. Evaluation Systems is the company commissioned by the California Commission on Teacher Credentialing (CTC) to help create, administer, and grade the RICA exam.

The RICA consists of two assessment options: A Written Exam and a Video Performance Assessment. Of the two, the Written Exam has a slightly higher pass rate. Between 2008 and 2013, 73.9% of examinees passed the Written Exam on the first attempt, with a 91.2% cumulative pass rate, but only 53.3% passed the Video Performance Assessment the first time, and 59.6% collectively. When combined, the two test versions have a 73.9% first-time pass rate and 91.5% cumulative pass rate. The number of candidates taking the RICA during 2012-2013 was 9,764, which is quite a bit less than the high of 26,000 in 2003-04.

Test Administration

The RICA Written Examination is given via a computer-based format by National Evaluation Systems, a division of Pearson Education, Inc. Once a candidate has registered for the RICA, appointments may be scheduled online at any time. Test appointments are accepted year-round on a first-come, first-served basis at Pearson VUE test centers throughout the world.

Individuals who choose to take the Video Performance Assessment version of the RICA need to create and send in a video recording exhibiting their reading instruction methods and techniques. Requirements for the video portion differ from year to year; therefore, video programs need to be created according to the instructions specific to that program year and cannot be carried over to consecutive years. The video portion requires a registration fee plus a submission fee. There are usually three of four Video Performance Assessment submission deadlines per year.

Individuals with physical, learning, or cognitive disabilities who demonstrate a need can request alternate arrangements with Pearson VUE. Test accommodations are personalized and decided on a per-case basis.

Test Format

The Written Portion and the Video Performance Assessment of the RICA exam both measure the same core competencies deemed necessary to successfully teach reading to students. These proficiencies are taken from the following five areas: planning, organizing, and managing reading instruction based on

ongoing assessment; word analysis; fluency; vocabulary, academic language, and background knowledge and comprehension.

The RICA Written Examination is structured as 70 multiple-choice questions, four constructed responses in essay format based on a specific reading situation, and one case study question based on the assessment of a student's reading performance (a typed response of about 300–600 words). Total test time is 4 hours, with 15 extra minutes allotted to fill out a nondisclosure agreement and take a tutorial. Time needed for breaks is subtracted from the existing testing time.

The RICA Video Performance Assessment allows candidates to be assessed on classroom teaching performance rather than taking a written test. Individuals who choose this format must produce and send in three video packages, each containing a teaching framework form, a 10-minute video, and a contemplation form. Requirements are often different from year to year, and therefore must be based on the guidelines in the RICA Video Performance Assessment Procedures Manual for that specific year.

Scoring

The score for the multiple-choice section on the RICA Written Exam is based on the number of questions answered correctly; there is no penalty for guessing. For the constructed-response questions, each answer is scored independently; the total of these two scores is computed as the raw score for that specific question. The raw scores for each answer are then weighted. The total score for the written portion is the sum of the score on the multiple-choice section plus the weighted score from the constructed responses. These two sections are translated into a scaled score. The case study is scored separately and makes up 20% of the total exam points.

Each of the three video portion packets is scored as a single entity. Two different individuals assess each packet. The raw score for each candidate is the total of the six scores obtained from the various scoring experts. The raw score is then translated into a scaled score.

The range of scores for both exams is 100-300. In order to successfully gain RICA certification, a passing score of at least 220 on either test format is required.

Recent/Future Developments

As of August 30, 2016, results for the RICA Written Exam are accessible via a candidate's account for 2 years (in the past, results were only available for 45 days). Test results for the RICA Video Performance Assessment can be accessed online via a PDF file for 45 days after the scores are released. Copies of test results can be requested by submitting a reprint request form once the 2-year timeframe is over (or in the case of the RICA Video Performance Assessment, the 45-day period).

Practice Test #1

Planning, Organizing, and Managing Reading Instruction Based on Ongoing Assessment Questions

1. It is important to choose a variety of texts to elicit higher-level thinking skills. Which of the following text groupings would be appropriate to reach this goal?
   a. Basal readers, fantasy texts, and sci-fi novels
   b. Nonfiction, fiction, cultural pieces, and United States documents
   c. Scholastic magazine articles
   d. Textbooks and high-interest blogs

2. Informational text should comprise what percentage of all text used in instruction by the time students reach the twelfth grade?
   a. 25 percent
   b. 55 percent
   c. 50 percent
   d. 70 percent

3. The RICA's content is organized into five domains. What is the first domain?
   a. Word analysis and vocabulary based on ongoing assessments
   b. Planning, organizing, and managing math assessment based on ongoing assessments
   c. Comprehension strategies
   d. Planning, organizing, and managing reading instruction based on ongoing assessments

4. A first grader that is in a classroom's reading center appears to be frustrated. How can the teacher best help this student find a book that is at the appropriate reading level?
   a. Have the student do a five-finger test for vocabulary
   b. Pick a new book for the student
   c. Have the student try to figure it out on their own
   d. Have a peer read the book to the student

5. Which element is important for a teacher to consider when planning a lesson?
   I. Pacing
   II. Intervention groups
   III. Modeling and direct instruction
   a. III only
   b. I and II
   c. I and III
   d. I, II, and III

6. What is an effective strategy when working with a child who has an Individualized Education Program (IEP)?

       I. Provide remediation during which the teacher works with the student on a particular skill

       II. Allow the student to work independently

       III. Chart the student's performance on a particular skill on a weekly basis in order to observe the student's growth over time

       a. II and III

       b. I and II

       c. I and III

       d. I, II, and III

7. Which best describes the areas included in the California English Language standards for reading instruction?

       a. Writing, language, speaking, and reading

       b. Reading and writing only

       c. Speaking and reading only

       d. Language development and reading only

8. What is the goal of a reading specialist position at a school site?

       I. To inform staff of changes in the curriculum

       II. To offer reading lessons in the classroom

       III. To instruct staff on how to do their job

       a. II only

       b. I and II

       c. II and III

       d. I, II, and III

9. Which of the following is NOT the best way to utilize a reading center or corner in a classroom?

       a. As a spot for students to play games

       b. As a private and quiet place to chat about books

       c. As a location to provide a variety of leveled readers

       d. As a place with fun and entertaining décor to enhance a comfortable learning environment

10. Which of the following is a guideline of reading instruction in California?

       a. Instruction should be templated.

       b. Instruction should be differentiated.

       c. Instruction should be offered without prior modeling.

       d. Instruction should be the same for each student.

Word Analysis

1. In the word *shut*, the *sh* is an example of what?

       a. Consonant digraph

       b. Sound segmentation

       c. Vowel digraph

       d. Rime

2. When students identify the phonemes in spoken words, they are practicing which of the following?
   a. Sound blending
   b. Substitution
   c. Rhyming
   d. Segmentation

3. What is the alphabetic principle?
   a. The understanding that letters represent sounds in words.
   b. The ability to combine letters to correctly spell words.
   c. The proper use of punctuation within writing.
   d. The memorization of all the letters in the alphabet.

4. Print awareness includes all EXCEPT which of the following concepts?
   a. The differentiation of uppercase and lowercase letters
   b. The identification of word boundaries
   c. The proper tracking of words
   d. The spelling of sight words

5. When teachers point to words during shared readings, what are they modeling?
   I. Word boundaries
   II. Directionality
   III. One-to-one correspondence
   a. I and II
   b. I and III
   c. II and III
   d. I, II, and III

6. Structural analysis would be the most appropriate strategy in determining the meaning of which of the following words?
   a. Extra
   b. Improbable
   c. Likely
   d. Wonder

7. A student spells *eagle* as *EGL*. This student is performing at which stage of spelling?
   a. Conventional
   b. Phonetic
   c. Semiphonetic
   d. Transitional

8. Spelling instruction should include which of the following?
   I. Word walls
   II. Daily reading opportunities
   III. Daily writing opportunities
   IV. Weekly spelling inventories with words students have studied during the week
   a. I and IV
   b. I, II, and III
   c. I, II, and IV
   d. I, II, III, and IV

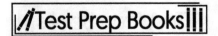

9. A kindergarten student is having difficulty distinguishing the letters *b* and *d*. The teacher should do which of the following?
    a. Have the student use a think-aloud to verbalize the directions of the shapes used when writing each letter.
    b. Have the student identify the letters within grade-appropriate texts.
    c. Have the student write each letter five times.
    d. Have the student write a sentence in which all of the letters start with either *b* or *d*.

10. When differentiating phonics instruction for English-language learners (ELLs), teachers should do which of the following?
    a. Increase the rate of instruction
    b. Begin with the identification of word boundaries
    c. Focus on syllabication
    d. Capitalize on the transfer of relevant skills from the learners' original language(s)

11. Which of the following is the most appropriate assessment of spelling for students who are performing at the pre-phonetic stage?
    a. Sight word drills
    b. Phonemic awareness tests
    c. Writing samples
    d. Concepts about print (CAP) test

12. Phonological awareness is best assessed through which of the following?
    a. Identification of rimes or onsets within words
    b. Identification of letter-sound correspondences
    c. Comprehension of an audio book
    d. Writing samples

13. The identification of morphemes within words occurs during the instruction of what?
    a. Structural analysis
    b. Syllabic analysis
    c. Phonics
    d. The alphabetic principle

14. Which of the following pairs of words are homophones?
    a. Playful and replay
    b. To and too
    c. Was and were
    d. Gloomy and sad

15. Nursery rhymes are used in kindergarten to develop what?
    a. Print awareness
    b. Phoneme recognition
    c. Syllabication
    d. Structural analysis

16. High-frequency words such as *be, the,* and *or* are taught during the instruction of what?
    a. Phonics skills
    b. Sight word recognition
    c. Vocabulary development
    d. Structural analysis

17. To thoroughly assess students' phonics skills, teachers should administer assessments that require students to do which of the following?
    a. Decode in context only
    b. Decode in isolation only
    c. Both A and B
    d. Neither A nor B

18. What is a morpheme?
    a. The smallest unit of sound in a language
    b. The sound produced by a single letter
    c. A unit of pronunciation with a single vowel
    d. The smallest meaningful unit of language

19. A student writes the sentence, "I lik to play soker," instead of, "I like to play soccer." What stage of spelling development has this student reached?
    a. Precommunicative spelling
    b. Semiphonetic spelling
    c. Phonetic spelling
    d. Conventional spelling

20. What is the difference between rhyme and rime?
    a. Rhyme is only used in teaching higher academic concepts in poetry and literature, while rime is an appropriate classroom topic for students of all ages.
    b. Rhyme refers to the repetition of ending sounds (usually the final vowel and consonant) regardless of spelling, while rime depends on both identical spelling and pronunciation.
    c. Rhyme is more applicable to everyday language usage, while rime is only encountered in the classroom.
    d. Rhyme is more effective for developing phonological awareness, while rime is more effective for developing spelling skills.

21. Which of the following is an example of a word with an initial consonant blend?
    a. Frame
    b. Chart
    c. Each
    d. Knife

22. A teacher asks a student, "What sound do you hear at the end of the word 'clock'?" What is the teacher assessing?
    a. The student's ability to apply syllabication
    b. The student's phonological awareness
    c. The student's grasp of the alphabetic principle
    d. The student's conventional spelling skills

23. In order to give students writing practice outside of the classroom, a teacher assigns them to write short journal entries based on their weekend activities. One student writes about her trip to the zoo and includes the following sentence in her journal entry: "I saw bunnys and butterflys at the zoo." Which of the following best explains the student's error?

    a. She has not yet mastered the orthographic rules for -y plurals.

    b. She has not had sufficient independent writing experience.

    c. She has not been exposed to enough reading materials about animals.

    d. She has not seen plurals in written form before; she has only heard them spoken.

24. During a read-aloud assessment, a student reads the word *cooked* with two syllables ("cook-ed"). Which of the following best explains the student's error?

    a. The student is unfamiliar with the content of the text and was unable to decode the word based on background knowledge.

    b. The student has underdeveloped syllabication skills.

    c. The student failed to recognize the inflectional morpheme.

    d. The student was confused because the word contains two different letters that represent the same phoneme, /k/.

Fluency

1. What contributes the most to schema development?

    a. Reading comprehension

    b. Structural analysis

    c. Written language

    d. Background knowledge

2. Which of the following is NOT an essential component of effective fluency instruction?

    a. Spelling

    b. Feedback

    c. Guidance

    d. Practice

3. The Directed-Reading Think-Aloud (DRTA) method helps students to do what?

    a. Build prior knowledge by exploring audiovisual resources before a reading

    b. Predict what will occur in a text and search the text to verify the predictions

    c. Identify, define, and review unfamiliar terms

    d. Understand the format of multiple types and genres of text

4. A teacher assigns a writing prompt in order to assess her students' reading skills. Which of the following can be said about this form of reading assessment?

    a. It is the most beneficial way to assess reading comprehension

    b. It is invalid because a student's ability to read and write are unrelated

    c. It is erroneous since the strength of a student's reading and writing vocabulary may differ

    d. It is the worst way to assess reading comprehension

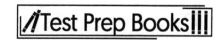
5. When does scaffolded reading occur?
    a. A student hears a recording of herself reading a text in order to set personal reading goals.
    b. A student receives assistance and feedback on strategies to utilize while reading from someone else.
    c. A student is given extra time to find the answers to predetermined questions.
    d. A student is pulled out of a class to receive services elsewhere.

6. What are the three interconnected indicators of reading fluency?
    a. Phonetics, word morphology, and listening comprehension
    b. Accuracy, rate, and prosody
    c. Syntax, semantics, and vocabulary
    d. Word exposure, phonetics, and decodable skills

7. Which of the following about effective independent reading is NOT true?
    a. Students should read texts that are below their reading levels during independent reading.
    b. Students need to first demonstrate fluency before reading independently.
    c. Students who don't yet display automaticity should whisper to themselves when reading aloud.
    d. Students who demonstrate automaticity in decoding should be held accountable during independent reading.

8. Timed oral reading can be used to assess which of the following?
    a. Phonics
    b. Listening comprehension
    c. Reading rate
    d. Background knowledge

Vocabulary, Academic Language, and Background Knowledge

1. A student is having difficulty pronouncing a word that she comes across when reading aloud. Which of the following is most likely NOT a reason for the difficulty that the student is experiencing?
    a. Poor word recognition
    b. A lack of content vocabulary
    c. Inadequate background knowledge
    d. Repeated readings

2. Which of the following is the largest contributor to the development of students' written vocabulary?
    a. Reading
    b. Directed reading
    c. Direct teaching
    d. Modeling

3. The study of roots, suffixes, and prefixes is called what?
    a. Listening comprehension
    b. Word consciousness
    c. Word morphology
    d. Textual analysis

4. A student's understanding of vocabulary found in a science textbook is most dependent upon which of the following?

    a. A knowledge of grammar

    b. Word morphology

    c. Graphics provided within the text

    d. Writing devices such as dialogue, description, and pacing

5. Word walls are used to do what?

        I. Allow students to share words they find interesting

        II. Present words utilized in a current unit of study

        III. Provide a barrier to independent reading

        IV. Specify words that students are to utilize within writing assignments

    a. I and II only

    b. I, II, and III

    c. I, II, and IV

    d. I, II, III, and IV

6. Context clues assist vocabulary development by providing what?

    a. A knowledge of roots, prefixes, and suffixes are used to determine the meaning a word

    b. Information within the sentence that surrounds an unknown word is used to determine the word's meaning

    c. Content learned in previous grades that serves as a bridge to the new term

    d. Background knowledge to fill in a missing word within a sentence

7. What can be used when a student comes across an unfamiliar word?

    a. Decoding skills

    b. Structural analysis

    c. Contextual clues

    d. Any of the above

8. A teacher writes a morpheme and its definition in the center of a word map, such as that displayed below.

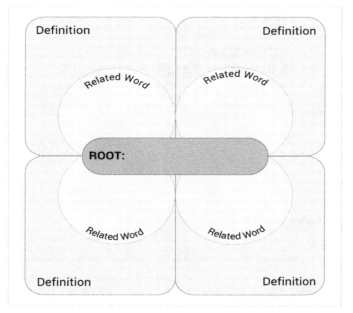

He then asks students to think of other English words that also contain the given morpheme. This activity is most likely to promote students' vocabulary development by helping them to do what?
    a. Apply concept mapping to show similarities and differences amongst a group of words
    b. Gain exposure to common affixes
    c. Determine the meaning of unknown words that contain a known morpheme
    d. Use phonics to determine the meaning of unknown words

9. A student writes the following in an essay:
    Protestors filled the streets of the city. Because they were dissatisfied with the government's leadership.

Which of the following is an appropriately-punctuated correction for this sentence?
    a. Protestors filled the streets of the city, because they were dissatisfied with the government's leadership.
    b. Protesters, filled the streets of the city, because they were dissatisfied with the government's leadership.
    c. Because they were dissatisfied with the government's leadership protestors filled the streets of the city.
    d. Protestors filled the streets of the city because they were dissatisfied with the government's leadership.

10. While studying vocabulary, a student notices that the words *circumference*, *circumnavigate*, and *circumstance* all begin with the prefix *circum–*. The student uses her knowledge of affixes to infer that all of these words share what related meaning?
    a. Around, surrounding
    b. Travel, transport
    c. Size, measurement
    d. Area, location

11. A student wants to rewrite the following sentence:

Entrepreneurs use their ideas to make money.

He wants to use the word *money* as a verb, but he isn't sure which word ending to use. What is the appropriate suffix to add to *money* to complete the following sentence?

Entrepreneurs _____ their ideas.

a. –ize
b. –ical
c. –en
d. –ful

12. A student reads the following sentence:

A hundred years ago, automobiles were rare, but now cars are ubiquitous.

However, she doesn't know what the word *ubiquitous* means. Which key context clue is essential to decipher the word's meaning?

a. Ago
b. Cars
c. Now
d. Rare

13. A local newspaper is looking for writers for a student column. A student would like to submit his article to the newspaper, but he isn't sure how to format his article according to journalistic standards. What resource should he use?
a. A thesaurus
b. A dictionary
c. A style guide
d. A grammar book

14. A student encounters the word *aficionado* and wants to learn more about it. It doesn't sound like other English words he knows, so the student is curious to identify the word's origin. What resource should he consult?
a. A thesaurus
b. A dictionary
c. A style guide
d. A grammar book

15. Which domain is likely to be used by a website run by a nonprofit group?
a. .com
b. .edu
c. .org
d. .gov

Comprehension

1. What type of texts are considered nonfiction?
   a. Folktales
   b. Memoirs
   c. Fables
   d. Short stories

2. What is a summative assessment?
   a. A formal assessment that is given at the end of a unit of study
   b. An informal assessment that is given at the end of a unit of study
   c. An assessment that is given daily and is usually only a few questions in length, based on the day's objective
   d. An assessment given at the end of the week that is usually based on observation

3. How are typographic features useful when teaching reading comprehension?
   a. Typographic features are graphics used to illustrate the story and help students visualize the text.
   b. Typographic features give the answers in boldfaced print.
   c. Typographic features are not helpful when teaching reading comprehension and should not be used.
   d. Typographic features are print in boldface, italics, and subheadings, used to display changes in topics or to highlight important vocabulary or content.

4. What do English Language Learners need to identify prior to comprehending text?
   a. Vocabulary
   b. Figurative language
   c. Author's purpose
   d. Setting

5. What kind of assessment is most beneficial for students with special needs?
   a. Frequent and ongoing
   b. Weekly
   c. Monthly
   d. Summative assessments only at the end of a unit of study

6. Which is NOT a reason that independent reading is important for developing reading comprehension?
   a. To develop a lifelong love of reading
   b. To encourage students to read a genre they enjoy
   c. So that students can read at their own pace
   d. To visit the reading corner, which is an area of the classroom that is restful and enjoyable

7. Why are purposeful read-alouds by a teacher important to enhance reading comprehension?
   a. They encourage students to unwind from a long day and reading lesson.
   b. They encourage students to listen for emphasis and voice.
   c. They encourage students to compare the author's purpose versus the teacher's objective.
   d. They encourage students to work on important work from earlier in the day while listening to a story.

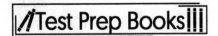
8. Which of the following is the study of what words mean in certain situations?
   a. Morphology
   b. Pragmatics
   c. Syntax
   d. Semantics

9. What is "text evidence" when referring to answering a comprehension question?
   a. Taking phrases directly from the text itself to answer a question
   b. Using a variety of resources to find the answer
   c. Using technology and websites to locate an answer
   d. Paraphrasing and using a student's own words to answer the question

10. The RICA for reading comprehension addresses which three of the listed comprehension areas?
   a. Objective, subjective, and inferential comprehension
   b. Nonfiction, fiction, and objective comprehension
   c. Literal, inferential, and evaluative comprehension
   d. Literal, inferential, and subjective comprehension

11. Why are group-based discussion MOST important in the classroom to enhance reading comprehension?
   a. They promote student discussions without the teacher present.
   b. They promote student discussions with a friend.
   c. They promote student discussions so that those who didn't understand the text can get answers from another student.
   d. They give all students a voice and allow them to share their answer, rather than one student sharing an answer with the class

12. Which of the following skills is NOT useful when initially helping students understand and comprehend a piece of text?
   a. Graphic organizers
   b. Note-taking
   c. Small intervention groups
   d. Extension projects and papers

13. Why are intervention groups important to advanced learners?
   a. They are not useful, as they do not need intervention in a particular skill
   b. They can be used to teach struggling students
   c. They can be given more advanced and complex work
   d. They can be given tasks to do in the classroom while others are meeting for intervention

Answer Explanations for Practice Test #1

Planning, Organizing, and Managing Reading Instruction Based on Ongoing Assessment Questions

1. B: California advocates that students become career and college ready. Doing so requires students to read a wide variety of literary and informational texts. Texts may extend across a wide variety of genres, timelines, and cultural works. Nonfiction, fiction, cultural pieces, and United States documents are all excellent examples of texts to use during reading instruction.

2. D: Students should be exposed to 70 percent of nonfiction text during reading instruction by the time they reach the twelfth grade. By eighth grade, students should be exposed to 55 percent of nonfiction text. Students should be exposed to a 50/50 balance from kindergarten to fifth grade.

3. D: The California RICA is divided into five domains. The first domain is to understand how to plan, organize, and manage standards-based reading instruction. The other domains include word analysis, fluency, vocabulary, academic language, and background knowledge and comprehension.

4. A: Young students should use the five-finger test to select an appropriate-level text. Using the five-finger test, a student selects a page within a text that they desire to read. The student holds up a finger for each word he or she is unable to read on that page. If the student has five fingers up after reading the entire page, then the student should stop and choose a book at an easier reading level. If there is not a variety of books of various reading levels from which a student can choose, then the student is likely to become frustrated. Such frustration may cause the student to stop reading for pleasure and see reading as a chore.

5. D: Elements of a good lesson are all of the above criteria. Pacing, modeling, direct instruction, and intervention are necessary to build a strong reading lesson. Teachers need to account for time given by a district for reading. That time should include whole-class instruction of new reading skills. Teachers should then assess students formatively during guided and independent practice in order to break students into groups based on their performance levels.

6. C: It is important for teachers to allocate time to work one-on-one with students who have IEPs. Students with IEPs may need to have skills retaught. Measuring the growth of students with IEPs can be done by charting their performance levels on a weekly basis. If there is little or no growth, a teacher may need to revisit their pacing or the form of instruction being used with the student(s).

7. A: Writing, language, speaking, and reading are all fundamental components needed for students to develop reading skills according to the California state reading standards. California state standards require the use of open-ended questions. Such assessments can be written or presented orally. Either way, students need to use textual evidence to support their responses. Therefore, good writing skills, language, and grammar development are essential.

8. B: The role of a reading specialist is not to tell teachers how to do their jobs, but rather to assist them. One role of a reading coach is to help teachers in their classrooms with assessing students or even teach lessons for teachers. Another role of a reading specialist is to inform staff of district changes at staff meetings, in-services, or in professional development opportunities. Such changes may include alterations of curriculum or state standards.

9. A: A reading corner is not designed to be a "hang out" for students. Rather, it is a place for students to share thoughts on books or discuss recommendations. A reading corner should have a fun atmosphere to enhance students' interest in reading and be filled with a variety of genres and levels.

10. B: Instruction should be differentiated. As students learn at different paces and levels, instruction should meet the needs of all students. This requires teachers to do ongoing assessments and group students according to these assessments. Grouping students may be based on needed skills or pacing of students.

Word Analysis

1. A: The *sh* is an example of a consonant digraph. Consonant digraphs are combinations of two or three consonants that work together to make a single sound. Examples of consonant digraphs are *sh*, *ch*, and *th*. Choice *B*, sound segmentation, is used to identify component phonemes in a word, such as separating the /t/, /u/, and /b/ for *tub*. Choice *C*, vowel digraph, is a set of two vowels that make up a single sound, such as *ow*, *ae*, or *ie*. Choice *D*, rime, is the sound that follows a word's onset, such as the /at/ in *cat*.

2. D: Sound segmentation is the identification of all the component phonemes in a word. An example would be the student identifying each separate sound, /t/, /u/, and /b/, in the word *tub*. Choice *A*, sound blending, is the blending together of two or more sounds in a word, such as /ch/ or /sh/. Choice *B*, substitution, occurs when a phoneme is substituted within a word for another phoneme, such as substituting the sound /b/ in *bun* to /r/ to create *run*. Choice *C*, rhyming, is an effective tool to utilize during the analytic phase of phonics development because rhyming words are often identical except for their beginning letters.

3. A: The alphabetical principle is the understanding that letters represent sounds in words. It is through the alphabetic principle that students learn the interrelationships between letter-sound (grapheme-phoneme) correspondences, phonemic awareness, and early decoding skills (such as sounding out and blending letter sounds).

4. D: Print awareness includes all except the spelling of sight words. Print awareness includes Choice *A*, the differentiation of uppercase and lowercase letters, so that students can understand which words begin a sentence. Choice *B*, the identification of word boundaries, is also included in print awareness; that is, students should be made aware that words are made up of letters and that spaces appear between words, etc. Choice *C*, the proper tracking of words, is also included in print awareness; this is the realization that print is organized in a particular way, so books must be tracked and held accordingly.

5. D: Word boundaries is included as one of the factors modeled because students should be able to identify which letters make up a word as well as the spaces before and after the letters that make up words. Directionality is the ability to track words as they are being read, so this is also modeled. One-to-one correspondence, the last factor listed, is the ability to match written letters to words to a spoken word when reading. It is another thing teachers model when they point to words while they read.

6. B: Structural analysis focuses on the meaning of morphemes. Morphemes include base words, prefixes, and word endings (inflections and suffixes) that are found within longer words. Students can use structural analysis skill to find familiar word parts within an unfamiliar word in order to decode the

word and determine the definition of the new word. The prefix im- (meaning not) in the word "improbable" can help students derive the definition of an event that is not likely to occur.

7. B: The student is performing at the phonetic stage. Phonetic spellers will spell a word as it sounds. The speller perceives and represents all of the phonemes in a word. However, because phonetic spellers have limited sight word vocabulary, irregular words are often spelled incorrectly.

8. B: The creation of word walls, Choice *I*, is advantageous during the phonetic stage of spelling development. On a word wall, words that share common consonant-vowel patterns or letter clusters are written in groups. Choices *II* and *III*, daily reading and writing opportunities, are also important in spelling instructions. Students need daily opportunities in order to review and practice spelling development. Daily journals or exit tickets are cognitive writing strategies effective in helping students reflect on what they have learned. A spelling inventory, Choice *IV*, is different than a traditional spelling test because students are not allowed to study the words prior to the administration of a spelling inventory. Therefore, this option is incorrect as it mentions the inventory contains words students have studied all week.

9. A: The teacher should have the student use a think-aloud to verbalize the directions of the shapes used when writing each letter. During think-alouds, teachers voice the metacognitive process that occurs when writing each part of a given letter. Students should be encouraged to do likewise when practicing writing the letters.

10. D: Teachers should capitalize on the transfer of relevant skills from the learner's original language(s). In this way, extra attention and instructional emphasis can be applied toward the teaching of sounds and meanings of words that are nontransferable between the two languages.

11. C: Writing samples are the most appropriate assessment of spelling for students who are performing at the pre-phonetic stage. During the pre-phonetic stage, students participate in precommunicative writing. Precommunicative writing appears to be a jumble of letter-like forms rather than a series of discrete letters. Samples of students' precommunicative writing can be used to assess their understanding of the alphabetic principle and their knowledge of letter-sound correspondences.

12. A: Phonological awareness is best assessed through identification of rimes or onsets within words. Instruction of phonological awareness includes detecting and identifying word boundaries, syllables, onset/rime, and rhyming words.

13. A: The identification of morphemes within words occurs during the instruction of structural analysis. Structural analysis is a word recognition skill that focuses on the meaning of word parts, or morphemes, during the introduction of a new word. Choice *B*, syllabic analysis, is a word analysis skill that helps students split words into syllables. Choice *C*, phonics, is the direct correspondence between and blending of letters and sounds. Choice *D*, the alphabetic principle, teaches that letters or other characters represent sounds.

14. B: Homophones are words that are pronounced the same way but differ in meaning and/or spelling. The pair *to* and *too* is an example of a homophone because they are pronounced the same way, but differ in both meaning and spelling. Choices *A*, *C*, and *D* are not homophones because they do not sound the same when spoken aloud.

15. B: Nursery rhymes are used in kindergarten to develop phoneme recognition. Rhyming words are often almost identical except for their beginning letter(s), so rhyming is a great strategy to implement during the analytic phase of phoneme development.

16. B: High-frequency words are taught during the instruction of sight word recognition. Sight words, sometimes referred to as high-frequency words, are words that are used often but may not follow the regular principles of phonics. Sight words may also be defined as words that students are able to recognize and read without having to sound out.

17. C: Both *A* and *B*. Decoding should be assessed in context in addition to isolation. During such assessments, the students read passages from reading-level appropriate texts aloud to the teacher so that the teacher is better able to analyze a student's approach to figuring out unknown words. Decoding should also be assessed in isolation. In these types of assessments, students are given a list of words and/or phonics patterns. Initially, high-frequency words that follow predictable phonics patterns are presented. The words that are presented become more challenging as a student masters less difficult words.

18. D: The smallest meaningful unit of language. A morpheme is the smallest unit of language that still contains meaning and cannot be broken down further. A word may be a single morpheme or several morphemes. For example, the word *horse* is a single morpheme, but the word *horseback* consists of two morphemes. The smallest unit of sound (Choice *A*) in a language is a phoneme, and a unit of pronunciation with a single vowel (Choice *C*) is a syllable, so those answers are incorrect.

19. C: The student's spelling demonstrates phonetic awareness, or the understanding that letters correlate to produced sounds. In precommunicative spelling (Choice *A*), a student may know how to write some letters but has not grasped how they correspond to sounds. As students develop their phonetic awareness, they begin using single letters (for example, *u* instead of *you*) and other simplified spellings. A student at the phonetic stage (Choice *C*) such as this recognizes, for example, that the letter *k* represents the phoneme /k/ and has used it to spell the word *soccer*. At the conventional spelling stage (Choice *D*), students are able to use correct spellings even when they do not follow standard phonetic rules.

20. B: Rhyme refers to the repetition of ending sounds (usually the final vowel and consonant) regardless of spelling, while rime depends on both identical spelling and pronunciation. Both rhyme and rime refer to the repetition of ending sounds, and both are useful in teaching word recognition, pronunciation, and orthographic patterns. However, words with ending rhymes may sound the same but use different spelling (for example, *tough* and *stuff*), whereas rimes will always have identical spelling (*stop* and *pop* or *song* and *long*).

21. A: A consonant blend occurs when two or more consonants are placed together to produce a combined pronunciation, but each individual consonant sound can still be heard. Therefore, the word *frame* contains a consonant blend. *Chart* (Choice *B*) and *knife* (Choice *D*) are not correct answers because, while each word does begin with two consonants, they are examples of digraphs, or combinations of two letters that create one new sound (that is, the *kn* in *knife* produces a single sound and is not pronounced with the individual phonemes /k/ and /n/). *Each* (Choice *C*) is not correct because it begins with a diphthong, or two vowels that combine into a single syllable.

22. B: The teacher is asking the student to isolate a single sound, or phoneme, in the context of a word. The understanding that words are made up of individual sounds is phonological awareness. Choice *A* is incorrect because syllabication is the division of words into syllables, or units of pronunciation with a

single vowel sound. Choice *C* is incorrect because the alphabetic principle is the understanding that letters (or graphemes) represent sounds (or phonemes); in this example, the teacher is asking the student to listen to a word rather than recognize it visually. Choice *D* is incorrect for the same reason.

23. A: She has not yet mastered the orthographic rules for *-y* plurals. Orthographic rules govern spelling conventions—in this case, the rule that words ending with *-y* preceded by a consonant change to an *-ies* ending in the plural form. She may have encountered such words in writing before, but she has not formalized the rule in her own writing yet.

24. C: The student failed to recognize the inflectional morpheme. An inflectional morpheme is one that changes the word form or tense, such as *-es* at the end of some plurals or, in this case, *-ed* for past tense. Because inflectional morphemes can affect pronunciation (for example, the name *Ed* is pronounced different from the past tense *-ed* found in *cooked*), failure to recognize them can lead to pronunciation errors such as the one in this example.

Fluency

1. D: A schema is a framework or structure that stores and retrieves multiple, interrelated learning elements as a single packet of knowledge. Children who have greater exposure to life events have greater schemas. Thus, students who bring extensive background knowledge to the classroom are likely to experience easier automation when reading. In this way, background knowledge and reading comprehension are directly related. Likewise, students who have greater background knowledge are able to learn a greater number of new concepts at a faster rate.

2. A: Practice is an essential component of effective fluency instruction. When teachers provide daily opportunities for students to learn words and utilize word-analysis skills, accuracy and rate will likely increase. Oral reading accompanied by guidance and feedback from teachers, peers, or parents has a significant positive impact on fluency. In order to be beneficial, such feedback needs to target specific areas in which students need improvement, as well as strategies that students can use in order to improve their areas of need. Such feedback increases students' awareness so that they can independently make needed modifications to improve fluency.

3. B: DRTA, or Directed Reading-Thinking Activity, incorporates both read-alouds and think-alouds. During a DRTA, students make predictions about what they will read in order to set a purpose for reading, give cognitive focus, and activate prior knowledge. Students use reading comprehension in order to verify their predictions.

4. C: There are five types of vocabulary: listening, speaking, written, sight, and meaning. Most often, listening vocabulary contains the greatest number of words. This is usually followed by speaking vocabulary, sight reading vocabulary, meaning vocabulary, and written vocabulary. Formal written language usually utilizes a richer vocabulary than everyday oral language. Thus, students show differing strengths in reading vocabulary and writing vocabulary. Likewise, a student's reading ability will most likely differ when assessed via a reading assessment versus a writing sample.

5. B: Scaffolded opportunities occur when a teacher helps students by giving them support, offering immediate feedback, and suggesting strategies. In order to be beneficial, such feedback needs to help students identify areas that need improvement. Much like oral reading feedback, this advice increases students' awareness so they can independently make needed modifications in order to improve fluency.

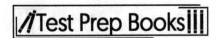

Scaffolding is lessened as the student becomes a more independent reader. Struggling readers, students with reading difficulties or disabilities, and students with special needs especially benefit from direct instruction and feedback that teaches decoding and analysis of unknown words, automaticity in key sight words, and correct expression and phrasing.

6. B: According to substandard 2 of RICA's Competency 8 Content Specification, key indicators of reading fluency include accuracy, rate, and prosody. Phonetics and decodable skills aid fluency. Syntax, semantics, word morphology, listening comprehension, and word exposure aid vocabulary development.

7. A: Once students become fluent readers, independent reading can begin. Students who don't yet display automaticity may need to read out loud or whisper to themselves during independent reading time. Independent silent reading accompanied by comprehension accountability is an appropriate strategy for students who demonstrate automaticity in their decoding skills. Also, each student should be provided with a text that matches his or her reading level.

8. C: The most common measurement of reading rate includes the oral contextual timed readings of students. During a timed reading, the number of errors made within a given amount of time is recorded. This data can be used to identify if a student's rate is improving and if the rate falls within the recommended fluency rates for their grade level.

Vocabulary, Academic Language, and Background Knowledge

1. D: An individual's sight vocabulary includes the words that he or she can recognize and correctly pronounce when reading. Limited sight vocabulary can be caused by poor word recognition, a lack of content vocabulary, and inadequate background knowledge. Although proper pronunciation may affect the ability to spell a word, the ability to properly spell a word is less likely to affect a student's ability to correctly pronounce that word.

2. A: There is a positive correlation between a student's exposure to text and the academic achievement of that individual. Therefore, students should be given ample opportunities to independently read as much text as possible in order to gain vocabulary and background knowledge.

3. C: By definition, morphology is the identification and use of morphemes such as root words and affixes. Listening comprehension refers to the processes involved in understanding spoken language. Word consciousness refers to the knowledge required for students to learn and effectively utilize language. Textual analysis is an approach that researchers use to gain information and describe the characteristics of a recorded or visual message.

4. B: Many terms in the sciences contain morphemes. For example, photosynthesis contains the morphemes "photo" and "synthesis." After being directly taught word morphology, students may be able to define an unfamiliar term by piecing together the meaning of the word's individual morphemes.

5. C: A love of words can be instilled when students share new and interesting words that they encounter through independent reading or that are taught by a teacher. These words can be kept in either word lists or word walls. Word lists and walls help to personalize vocabulary instruction while improving students' flexibility and fluency. Additionally, there are thousands of online word blogs and word clouds that encourage students to share the words they love. If a lack of technology is an issue, students can share new words on a word bank displayed on a wall within the classroom or a word list contained within a notebook. The list of new words should be referred to often in order to

increase students' exposure to new words. Students should be required to utilize the words within writing activities and discussions.

6. B: When using contextual strategies, students are indirectly introduced to new words within a sentence or paragraph. Contextual strategies require students to infer the meaning(s) of new words. Word meaning is developed by utilizing semantic and contextual clues of the reading in which the word is located.

7. D: When reading, multiple strategies are used to decode and interpret the meaning of an unfamiliar word. Phonetics allows students to sound out the word. Structural analysis can be used to combine word parts in order to decode an unfamiliar term. Students can also use contextual clues within the sentence or paragraph that surround the unfamiliar term in order to derive its definition.

8. C: Word maps are visual organizers that promote structural analysis skills for vocabulary development. Word maps may be used to relate words that share a common morpheme. After being directly taught word morphology, students may be able to define an unfamiliar term by piecing together the meaning of the word's individual morphemes. In this way, word maps enable students to build upon background knowledge in order to gain comprehension of new words.

9. D: The problem in the original passage is that the second sentence is a dependent clause that cannot stand alone as a sentence; it must be attached to the main clause found in the first sentence. Because the main clause comes first, it does not need to be separated by a comma. However, if the dependent clause came first, then a comma would be necessary, which is why Choice *C* is incorrect. Choices *A* and *B* also insert unnecessary commas into the sentence.

10. A: The affix *circum–* originates from Latin and means "around or surrounding." It is also related to other round words, such as *circle* and *circus*. The rest of the choices do not relate to the affix *circum–* and are therefore incorrect.

11. A: Only two of these suffixes, *–ize* and *–en*, can be used to form verbs, so Choices *B* and *D* are incorrect. Those choices create adjectives. The suffix *–ize* means "to convert or turn into." The suffix *–en* means "to become." Because this sentence is about converting ideas into money, money + *–ize* or *monetize* is the most appropriate word to complete the sentence, so Choice *C* is incorrect.

12. D: Students can use context clues to make a careful guess about the meaning of unfamiliar words. Although all of the words in a sentence can help contribute to the overall sentence, in this case, the adjective that pairs with *ubiquitous* gives the most important hint to the student—cars were first *rare*, but now they are *ubiquitous*. The inversion of *rare* is what gives meaning to the rest of the sentence and *ubiquitous* means "existing everywhere" or "not rare." Choice *A* is incorrect because *ago* only indicates a time frame. Choice *B* is incorrect because *cars* does not indicate a contrasting relationship to the word *ubiquitous* to provide a good context clue. Choice *C* is incorrect because it also only indicates a time frame, but used together with *rare*, it provides the contrasting relationship needed to identify the meaning of the unknown word.

13. C: A style guide offers advice about proper formatting, punctuation, and usage when writing for a specific field, such as journalism or scientific research. The other resources would not offer similar information. A dictionary is useful for looking up definitions; a thesaurus is useful for looking up synonyms and antonyms. A grammar book is useful for looking up specific grammar topics. Thus, Choices *A*, *C*, and *D* are incorrect.

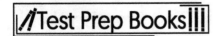
14. B: A word's origin is also known as its *etymology*. In addition to offering a detailed list of a word's various meanings, a dictionary also provides information about a word's history, such as when it first came into use, what language it originated from, and how its meaning may have changed over time. A thesaurus is for identifying synonyms and antonyms, so *A* is incorrect. A style guide provides formatting, punctuation, and syntactical advice for a specific field, and a grammar book is related to the appropriate placement of words and punctuation, which does not provide any insight into a word's meaning. Therefore, Choices *A*, *C*, and *D* are incorrect.

15. C: The .org domain on websites is generally used by nonprofit groups or community organizations. A government website uses .gov, and .edu is used for educational institutions. Private companies and businesses use .com, so Choices *A*, *B*, and *D* are incorrect.

Comprehension

1. B: Nonfiction texts include memoirs, biographies, autobiographies, and journalism. Choices *A*, *C*, and *D* are all examples of fictional prose.

2. A: Summative assessments are formal assessments that are given at the end of a unit of study. These assessments are usually longer in length. They are not completed daily. These summative assessments shouldn't be confused with informal assessments, which are used more frequently to determine mastery of the day's objective. However, summative assessments may be used to determine students' mastery, in order to form intervention groups thereafter.

3. D: Typographic features are important when teaching reading comprehension as the boldfaced, highlighted, or italics notify a student when a new vocabulary word or idea is present. Subtitles and heading can also alert a student to a change in topic or idea. These features are also important when answering questions, as a student may be able to easily find the answer with these typographic features present.

4. A: English Language Learners should master vocabulary and words in order to fully comprehend text. Figurative language, an author's purpose, and settings are more complex areas and are difficult for English Language Learners. These areas can be addressed once ELL students understand the meaning of words. In order to master comprehension skills, vocabulary and the English language need to be mastered first, but comprehension can still be difficult. Figurative language is culture-based, and inferences may be difficult for those with a different cultural background.

5. A: Assessments should always be frequent and ongoing for all students, but especially for those with special needs. These assessments may be informal, but given daily after direct instruction and modeling. Summative assessments are important, but this should not be the first and only assessment during a unit of study, as these types of assessments are given at the end of a unit of study. Weekly and monthly assessments are not frequent enough for instructors to identify struggling areas and for successful remediation and intervention.

6. D: Although the reading corner should be a restful and enjoyable place to encourage students to read independently, it does not enhance reading comprehension directly. Choices *A*, *B*, and *C* all encourage enhancement of reading comprehension. Giving students a chance to read independently allows them to choose books they enjoy, read at their own pace, and develop a lifelong enjoyment of reading.

7. B: Purposeful teacher read-alouds allow students to listen to a story for voice emphasis and tone. This will help students when they are reading independently as well. Although students may find this time

restful or a chance to catch up on old work, this is not the main purpose. Students may use this time to take notes on the reading, but students should only be listening to the story being read and not doing other work.

8. B: Pragmatics is the study of what words mean in certain situations. Choice *A*, morphology, involves the structure and formation of words. Choice *C*, syntax, refers to the order of words in a sentence. Choice *D*, semantics, addresses the distinct meanings of words.

9. A: "Text evidence" refers to taking phrases and sentences directly from the text and writing them in the answer. Students are not asked to paraphrase, nor use any other resources to address the answer. Therefore, Choices *B*, *C*, and *D* are incorrect.

10. C: The RICA for reading comprehension addresses the understanding of literal, inferential, and evaluative comprehension and various factors affecting reading comprehension. Nonfiction and fiction pieces are used on the RICA to address comprehension skills for the different text types such as reference documents, literature, and expository texts.

11. D: Text-based discussion, like think-pair-share, encourage all students to speak rather than having just one student share an answer. Each student is given time to collaborate with another student and share their thoughts. It is not intended for one student to give another student the answers, which is why Choice *C* is incorrect. Although Choices *A* and *B* might be correct, they are not the MOST important reason that text-based discussions are useful in the classroom.

12. D: Extension projects and papers should be used to challenge advanced learners, not learners developing comprehension skills. Graphic organizers, taking notes, and small intervention groups can aid in reading comprehension. Graphic organizers and taking notes are great ways for a student to outline key parts of the text. Small intervention groups set up by the instructor can then focus on individual needs.

13. C: Advanced students can benefit from intervention groups by allowing the students to be challenged with more complex assignments. These assignments can be worked on independently and can include more difficult questions or higher level vocabulary. Even short projects may be beneficial for these advanced students to work on throughout the week.

Practice Test #2

Planning, Organizing, and Managing Reading Instruction Based on Ongoing Assessment

1. Rating scales, student logs, and the POWER method are effective assessment practices for what area of literacy development?
   a. Reading
   b. Writing
   c. Spelling
   d. Listening

2. Volume, articulation, and awareness of audience help with what practice?
   a. Effective instruction
   b. Communication
   c. Active listening
   d. Oral presentations

3. Offering a presenter with undivided attention and asking relevant and timely questions are examples of what skill set?
   a. Active listening skills
   b. Effective speaking
   c. Formal communication
   d. Informal communication

4. What is the method called that teachers use before and after reading to improve critical thinking and comprehension?
   a. Self-monitoring comprehension
   b. KWL charts
   c. Metacognitive skills
   d. Directed reading-thinking activities

5. When a student looks back at a previous reading section for information, he or she is using which of the following?
   a. Self-monitoring comprehension
   b. KWL charts
   c. Metacognitive skills
   d. Directed reading-thinking activities

6. Which choice of skills is NOT part of Bloom's Taxonomy?
   a. Remembering and understanding
   b. Applying and analyzing
   c. Listening and speaking
   d. Evaluating and creating

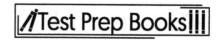

7. Predicting, Summarizing, Questioning, and Clarifying are steps of what?
    a. Reciprocal teaching
    b. Comprehensive teaching
    c. Activation teaching
    d. Summative teaching

8. When a student asks, "What do I know?" "What do I want to know?" and "What have I learned?" and records the answers in a table, he or she is using which of the following?
    a. Self-monitoring comprehension
    b. KWL charts
    c. Metacognitive skills
    d. Directed reading-thinking activities

9. Phonemic Awareness, Phonics, Fluency, Vocabulary, and Comprehension are the five basic elements of what?
    a. Bloom's Taxonomy
    b. Spelling instruction
    c. Reading education
    d. Genre

10. A teacher wants to help her students write a nonfiction essay on how the Pueblos built their homes. Before they write, she helps the students make clay from cornstarch and water, draw a plan for the house with a ruler, and build it using the clay and leaves from the schoolyard. These exercises are examples of what?
    a. Proficiency
    b. Collaboration
    c. Constructive writing
    d. Cross-curricular integration

Word Analysis

1. When children begin to negotiate the sounds that make up words in their language independently, what skill/s are they demonstrating?
    a. Phonological awareness
    b. Phonemes
    c. Phoneme substitution
    d. Blending skills

2. What is phonics?
    a. The study of syllabication
    b. The study of onsets and rimes
    c. The study of sound-letter relationships
    d. The study of graphemes

3. Word analysis skills are NOT critical for the development of what area of literacy?
    a. Vocabulary
    b. Reading fluency
    c. Spelling
    d. Articulation

4. How do the majority of high-frequency sight words differ from decodable words?
   a. They do not rhyme.
   b. They do not follow the Alphabetic Principle.
   c. They do not contain onsets.
   d. They contain rimes.

5. What developmental stage of writing are children demonstrating when they begin to leave spaces between words with a mixture of uppercase and lowercase letters?
   a. Emergence of beginning sound
   b. Strings of letters
   c. Words represented by consonants
   d. Transitional phase

6. When a student looks at a word and is able to tell the teacher that the letters spell C-A-T, but the student cannot actually say the word, what is the spelling stage of the student?
   a. Alphabetic Spelling
   b. Within Word Pattern Spelling
   c. Derivational Relations Spelling
   d. Emergent Spelling

7. A student is trying to read the word "preferred." She first recognizes the word "red" at the end, then sounds out the rest of the word by breaking it down into "pre," then "fer," then "red." Finally she puts it together and says "preferred." This student is displaying what attribute?
   a. Phonemic awareness
   b. Phonics
   c. Fluency
   d. Vocabulary

8. What allows readers to effectively translate print into recognizable speech?
   a. Fluency
   b. Spelling
   c. Phonics
   d. Word decoding

9. What is the most valuable strategy for helping children understand new words?
   a. Phonics instruction
   b. Pre-teaching
   c. Self-monitoring
   d. Context clues

10. A teacher wants to give students additional practice with visually similar letters, so he picks a story book that focuses on the letters *b* and *p*. The story includes repetition of pairs like *bat/pat, big/pig,* and *bin/pin*. After reading the story together, the teacher wants to select a supplementary activity to reinforce the skill. Which of the following would be the most useful activity?
   a. Have students practice writing the focus words from the story, but this time using capital letters.
   b. Put students into small groups to play a matching game, where each target word appears on two different cards and students have to recognize the words to make pairs.
   c. Have students brainstorm new words using the same rime but different onsets, such as *cat/sat/mat*.

d. Ask for volunteers to retell the story from memory to the class.

11. Which of the following is NOT an example of a category of function words?
   a. Determiners
   b. Auxiliary verbs
   c. Pronouns
   d. Adverbs

12. A first-grade class is preparing an end-of-year talent show that will be attended by parents and other family members. At the end of the show, all of the students say, "Thank you, Mom and Dad!" However, during rehearsals, one English learner always says, "Tank you, Mom and Dad." Which of the following most likely accounts for his delivery of the word *thank*?
   a. His native language lacks the corresponding onset phoneme.
   b. He does not recognize the individual letters in the digraph.
   c. He needs more practice with consonant blends.
   d. He has not mastered the alphabetic principle.

13. Which of the following is an example of a word that ends with a continuous sound?
   a. Bought
   b. Created
   c. Passes
   d. Picnic

14. A second-grade teacher places students into small groups and gives each group a chart of a dozen different words, including *hippo, classroom, snowing,* and *bookshelf*. She then asks students to identify which words are compound words. What is she assessing through this activity?
   a. Students' ability to decode words based on their knowledge of morphemes
   b. Students' familiarity with grade-level vocabulary
   c. Students' ability to use prefixes and suffixes
   d. Students' knowledge of blending

15. A teacher conducts a miscue analysis by having a student read the following: "Schools around the globe have different types of recess for students. Some schools have structured time for supervised athletic activities, and other schools give students free time to chat with friends." When the student reads the sentences, she produces the following: "Schools around the world have different types of recess for students. Some schools have structured time for supervised athletic activities, and other schools give students free time to talk with friends." What type of word error would the teacher identify?
   a. Syntactic
   b. Visual
   c. Semantic
   d. Graphophonemic

16. Which of the following is an example of a pair of homophones?
   a. Look, book
   b. So, sew
   c. Lead, lead
   d. Kayak, radar

17. What are the two types of morphemes?
    a. Free and bound
    b. Prefixes and suffixes
    c. Greek and Latin
    d. Affixes and inflections

18. Which of the following words would be most suited to structural analysis?
    a. Familiarity
    b. Allowance
    c. Indestructible
    d. Sincere

19. Which of the following is an example of a word with an *r*-controlled vowel?
    a. Root
    b. Cart
    c. Trust
    d. Rain

20. How do *r*-controlled vowels differ from other vowels?
    a. They can only appear at the middle or end of a word.
    b. They are formed by single vowels, not diphthongs.
    c. They are neither long nor short.
    d. They always make the schwa sound.

21. Which of the following is an example of a CVC word?
    a. Pop
    b. See
    c. Are
    d. Oak

22. A teacher asks students to read the word *cup* and then replace /p/ with /t/ to form a new word. What activity is the teacher conducting?
    a. Sound deletion
    b. Sound substitution
    c. Sound segmentation
    d. Sound blending

23. A teacher shows the sentence, "The sky is blue," to students before reading it aloud and then asking them to identify how many words are in the sentence. What skill is the teacher assessing?
    a. Syllabication
    b. Morphological awareness
    c. Automaticity
    d. Word awareness

24. A student who has a strong grasp of monosyllabic words is struggling to understand multisyllabic words. How can the teacher help the student develop her syllable awareness skills?
a. Have the student incorporate physical motion when she reads multisyllabic words, such as clapping or tapping the desk to count syllables.
b. Have the student write a list of target words and then draw lines for her to indicate syllable breaks in each word.
c. Show her how to use the dictionary to locate a word's pronunciation and syllable divisions.
d. Explain that each syllable has a single vowel sound.

Fluency

1. What area of study involves mechanics, usage, and sentence formation?
a. Word analysis
b. Spelling conventions
c. Morphemes
d. Phonics

2. Reading fluency involves what key areas?
a. Accuracy, rate, and prosody
b. Accuracy, rate, and consistency
c. Prosody, accuracy, and clarity
d. Rate, prosody, and comprehension

3. A child reads the story *Little Red Riding Hood* aloud. He easily pronounces the words, uses an apprehensive tone to show that the main character should not be leaving the path, adds a scary voice for the Big Bad Wolf, and reads the story at a pace that engages the class. What are these promising signs of?
a. Reading fluency
b. Phonemic awareness
c. Reading comprehension
d. Working memory

4. Poems are often an effective device when teaching what skill?
a. Fluency
b. Spelling
c. Writing
d. Word decoding

5. Syntax is best described as what?
a. The arrangement of words into sentences
b. The study of language meaning
c. The study of grammar and language structure
d. The proper formatting of a written text

6. What do informal reading assessments allow that standardized reading assessments do NOT allow?
a. The application of grade-level norms towards a student's reading proficiency
b. Personalization so that instruction can be differentiated based on each student's needs
c. The avoidance of partialities in the interpretation of reading assessments
d. The comparison of an individual's reading performance to that of other students in the class

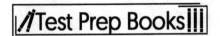

7. When building a class library, a teacher should be cognizant of the importance of what?
   a. Providing fiction that contains concepts relating to the background knowledge of all students in the class.
   b. Utilizing only nonfictional text that correlates to state and national standards in order to reinforce academic concept knowledge.
   c. Utilizing a single genre of text in order to reduce confusion of written structures.
   d. Including a wide range of fiction and nonfiction texts at multiple reading levels.

8. Samantha is in second grade and struggles with fluency. Which of the following strategies is likely to be most effective in improving Samantha's reading fluency?
   a. The teacher prompts Samantha when she pauses upon coming across an unknown word when reading aloud.
   b. The teacher records Samantha as she reads aloud.
   c. The teacher reads a passage out loud several times to Samantha and then has Samantha read the same passage.
   d. The teacher uses read-alouds and verbalizes contextual strategies that can be used to identify unfamiliar words.

Vocabulary, Academic Language, and Background Knowledge

1. The following is an example of what type of sentence?
   Although I wished it were summer, I accepted the change of seasons, and I started to appreciate the fall.

   a. Compound
   b. Simple
   c. Complex
   d. Compound-Complex

2. Read the following passage to answer the question below:
   The teacher directed the children's attention to the diagram, but the children couldn't understand the information.

   This is an example of what type of sentence?
   a. Complex
   b. Compound
   c. Simple
   d. Compound-Complex

3. Read the following sentences to answer the question below:
   Give me a shout back when you can.

   Please return my call at your earliest convenience.

   What is the main difference in these two sentences?
   a. Point of view
   b. Dialect
   c. Accent
   d. Register

4. What are the three tiers of vocabulary?
   a. Conversational, academic, and domain-specific language
   b. Informal, formal, and academic
   c. Social, professional, and academic
   d. Phonics, fluency, and rate

5. A teacher asks a student to describe a beautiful day. The student says the flowers were pretty, the air was warm, and animals were running. The teacher asks the student to specify how many flowers there were—just a few hopeful buds or an abundance of blossoms? Was the air still or breezy? How did it feel? The teacher is developing which trait in the student?
   a. Voice
   b. Word choice
   c. Organization
   d. Presentation

6. Writing practice for the sole purpose of communicating refers to what kind of writing?
   a. Persuasive
   b. Informational
   c. Narrative
   d. Purposeful

7. Speaking, listening, reading, and writing are four essential elements of what?
   a. Developmentally appropriate practice
   b. The Abecedarian Approach
   c. Literacy development
   d. Task, purpose, and audience

8. Synonyms, antonyms, and homonyms are examples of what?
   a. Syntax relationships
   b. Pragmatic relationships
   c. Semantic relationships
   d. Morphology relationships

9. Several generations ago, immigrants and locals in a region developed a simplified mixture of their two languages in order to carry out basic communication tasks. However, usage of this mixed language increased, and later generations passed it down to their children as their first language. These children are now speaking what kind of language?
   a. A pidgin
   b. A Creole
   c. A jargon
   d. A regionalism

10. Which of the following is true of Standard English?
   a. It is one dialect of English.
   b. It is the original form of English.
   c. It is the most complex form of English.
   d. It is the form that follows grammatical rules.

11. A teacher notices that when students are talking to each other between classes, they are using their own unique vocabulary words and expressions to talk about their daily lives. When the teacher hears these non-standard words that are specific to one age or cultural group, what type of language is she listening to?

    a. Slang
    b. Jargon
    c. Dialect
    d. Vernacular

12. A teacher wants to counsel a student about using the word *ain't* in a research paper for a high school English class. What advice should the teacher give?

    a. *Ain't* is not in the dictionary, so it isn't a word.
    b. Because the student isn't in college yet, *ain't* is an appropriate expression for a high school writer.
    c. *Ain't* is incorrect English and should not be part of a serious student's vocabulary because it sounds uneducated.
    d. *Ain't* is a colloquial expression, and while it may be appropriate in a conversational setting, it is not standard in academic writing.

13. A ninth-grade class is reading a novel together. After each chapter, they have a class discussion where students take turns summarizing the plot, sharing observations and reactions, and answering questions posed by the teacher. One question the teacher asks is, "How would you describe the diction in the text?" What is the teacher referring to?

    a. The unknown words students encounter in the text and want to learn
    b. The author's use of specific language in foreshadowing
    c. The words students recognize from earlier vocabulary instruction
    d. The author's word choice that contributes to the style and mood

14. A teacher asks his students to keep a class notebook during the semester. The notebook includes a section where they self-evaluate their study habits and identify areas they can improve. What is the main skill the teacher is targeting through this activity?

    a. Organization
    b. Daily writing habits
    c. Metacognition
    d. Test preparation

15. What are the three key factors to consider when selecting appropriate vocabulary terms for a class?

    a. Frequency, utility, and students' level of knowledge
    b. Etymology, spelling difficulty, and academic usage
    c. Word families, affixes, and common roots
    d. Literary, academic, and everyday

Comprehension

1. When students study character development, setting, and plot, what are they studying?

    a. Word analysis
    b. Points of view
    c. Literary analysis of a text
    d. Fluency

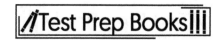
2. The author's purpose, major ideas, supporting details, visual aids, and vocabulary are the five key elements of what type of text?
   a. Fictional texts
   b. Narratives
   c. Persuasive texts
   d. Informational texts

3. When students use inference, what are they able to do?
   a. Make logical assumptions based on contextual clues
   b. Independently navigate various types of text
   c. Summarize a text's main idea
   d. Paraphrase a text's main idea

4. Story maps, an effective instructional tool, do NOT help children in what way?
   a. Analyze relationships among characters, events, and ideas in literature
   b. Understand key details of a story
   c. Follow the story's development
   d. Read at a faster pace

5. Which text feature does NOT help a reader locate information in printed or digital text?
   a. Hyperlink
   b. Sidebar
   c. Glossary
   d. Heading

6. Read the following sentences to answer the question below:

   He is a kind and generous man who wants nothing more than the best for his community, thought Michael as the board members discussed the nominees for head of council. Lana June, however, was far more critical. *He is just saying those things to get elected,* she thought.

What is the author's point of view?
   a. First person
   b. Third person limited
   c. Third person omniscient
   d. Objective

7. Autobiographies and memoirs are examples of what form of writing?
   a. Fiction
   b. Narrative
   c. Informational text
   d. Research papers

8. Which effective writing area engages and connects with the audience, igniting emotion?
   a. Ethos
   b. Logos
   c. Pathos
   d. Kairos

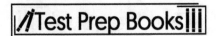

9. First-hand accounts of an event, subject matter, time period, or person are referred to as what type of source?
    a. Primary sources
    b. Secondary sources
    c. Direct sources
    d. Indirect sources

10. What type of literary device is being used in this sentence?
        I worked a billion hours this week!

    a. Idiom
    b. Metaphor
    c. Hyperbole
    d. Alliteration

11. What technique might an author use to let the reader know that the main character was in a car crash as a child?
    a. Point of view
    b. Characterization
    c. Figurative language
    d. Flashback

12. A graphic organizer is a method of achieving what?
    a. Integrating knowledge and ideas
    b. Generating questions
    c. Determining point of view
    d. Determining the author's purpose

13. A teacher is about to read a story. He tells the class they will be quizzed and need to pay attention. He instructs them to focus by clearing everything else from their desks, to look at his face for clues about the story's tone, and to think about the adjectives used to describe the characters to learn more about them. What skill is he teaching?
    a. Writing
    b. Reading
    c. Speaking
    d. Listening

Answer Explanations for Practice Test #2

Planning, Organizing, and Managing Reading Instruction Based on Ongoing Assessment

1. B: There are several effective assessments to evaluate a child's overall writing progress. Rating scales, student logs, and the POWER method are just some of these assessment methods. Although educators can create rating scales and student logs to assess and help students assess reading and spelling, the POWER method is specific to writing:

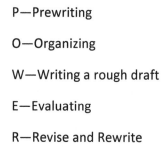

P—Prewriting

O—Organizing

W—Writing a rough draft

E—Evaluating

R—Revise and Rewrite

2. D: In order for oral presentations to be effective, the presenter's volume should match the size of the audience and the location of the presentation. The presenter should also practice articulation—how clearly the words are being said. The third most important element of oral presentations is how well the presenter is engaging the audience. Making eye contact, moving around the room, and involving the audience, when appropriate, are all part of audience awareness skills.

3. A: Active listening skills are very important in all forms of communication, whether one is at home, among friends, in school, or at work. An active listener is one who pays close attention to what is being said, maintains eye contact, uses body language to indicate respect, asks relevant questions, and shares information that directly pertains to the subject.

4. D: Teachers use directed reading-thinking activities before and after reading to improve critical thinking and reading comprehension. Metacognitive skills are when learners think about their thinking. Self-monitoring is when children are asked to think as they read and ask themselves if what they have just read makes sense. KWL charts help guide students to identify what they already know about a given topic.

5. C: Asking oneself a comprehension question is a metacognition skill. Readers with metacognitive skills have learned to think about thinking. It gives students control over their learning while they read. KWL charts help students to identify what they already know about a given topic.

6. C: Listening and speaking are not part of Bloom's Taxonomy. The six parts are remembering, understanding, applying, analyzing, evaluating, and creating.

7. A: Reciprocal teaching involves predicting, summarizing, questioning, and clarifying. The other choices are all fictitious.

8. B: KWL charts are an effective method of activating prior knowledge and taking advantage of students' curiosity. Students can create a KWL (*Know/Want to know/Learned*) chart to prepare for any unit of instruction and to generate questions about a topic.

9. C: The five basic components of reading education are phonemic awareness, phonics, fluency, vocabulary, and comprehension.

10. D: Cross-curricular integration is choosing to teach writing projects that include the subjects of science, social studies, mathematics, reading, etc.

Word Analysis

1. A: Phonological Awareness refers to a child's ability to understand and use familiar sounds in his or her social environment in order to form coherent words. Phonemes are defined as distinct sound units in any given language. Phonemic substitution is part of phonological awareness—a child's ability to substitute specific phonemes for others. Blending skills refers to the ability to construct or build words from individual phonemes by blending the sounds together in a unique sequence.

2. C: When children begin to recognize and apply sound-letter relationships independently and accurately, they are demonstrating a growing mastery of phonics. Phonics is the most commonly used method for teaching people to read and write by associating sounds with their corresponding letters or groups of letters, using a language's alphabetic writing system. Syllabication refers to the ability to break down words into their individual syllables. The study of onsets and rimes strives to help students recognize and separate a word's beginning consonant or consonant-cluster sound—the onset—from the word's rime—the vowel and/or consonants that follow the onset. A grapheme is a letter or a group of letters in a language that represent a sound.

3. D: Breaking down words into their individual parts, studying prefixes, suffixes, root words, rimes, and onsets are all examples of word analysis. When children analyze words, they develop their vocabulary and strengthen their spelling and reading fluency.

4. B: Although some high-frequency sight words are decodable, the majority of them are not. This means they do not follow the Alphabetic Principle, which relies on specific letter-sound correspondence. High-frequency sight words appear often in children's literature and are studied and memorized in order to strengthen a child's spelling and reading fluency. High-frequency sight words, as well as decodable words, may or may not rhyme and may or may not contain onsets and rimes.

5. C: There are eight developmental writing stages:

- Scribbling
- Letter-like symbols
- Strings of letters
- The emergence of beginning sounds
- Words represented by consonants
- Initial, middle, and final sounds
- Transitional phase
- Standard spelling

When children begin to leave visible spacing between words, even if those words are incorrectly spelled or if there is a mixture of upper and lower case letters, they are considered to be at the *Words represented by consonants* stage.

6. D: During the Emergent Spelling stage, children can identify letters but not the corresponding sounds. The other choices are all fictitious.

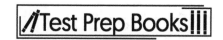

7. B: Phonics is the ability to apply letter-sound relationships and letter patterns in order to accurately pronounce written words. Phonemic awareness is the understanding that words are comprised of a combination of sounds. Fluency is an automatic recognition and accurate interpretation of text. Vocabulary is the body of words known to a person.

8. C: Phonics allows readers to effectively translate print into recognizable speech. If children lack proficiency in phonics, their ability to read fluently and to increase vocabulary will be limited.

9. B: Pre-teaching is the most valuable strategy for helping children understand new words. Educators select what they evaluate to be the unfamiliar words in the text and then introduce them to the class before reading. Educators using this method should be careful not to simply ask the children to read the text and then spell the new words correctly.

10. B: Put students into small groups to play a matching game where each target word appears on two different cards and students have to recognize the words to make pairs. In this situation, the teacher wants students to focus on the difference between the similar letter shapes *b* and *p*. The matching game requires students to pay attention to the form of the letters and also allows students to practice recognizing and reading the same words they have just heard in the story. Choice *A* is not the best answer because the capital letters *B* and *P* do not require the same type of differentiation as their lowercase forms. Choice *C* is appropriate for allowing students to connect new words with ones they already know but does not reinforce the target lesson. Choice *D* is also a way to assess comprehension, but again, does not target the specific *b* and *p* skill.

11. D: Adverbs are not a category of function words. Function words are contrasted with content words. While content words convey the unique meanings of the sentence, function words serve largely grammatical roles to help structure the sentence. For example, words such as *destroy, daily,* and *warm* are content words, while words such as *the, to,* and *can* are function words. Function words include words such as determiners (Choice *A*), auxiliary verbs (Choice *B*), pronouns (Choice *C*), and prepositions.

12. A: His native language lacks the corresponding onset phoneme. The phoneme /th/ does not appear in many languages, so English Language Learners may replace it with /s/ or /t/. Students may be able to recognize the phoneme even if they cannot produce it, so Choices *B* is not the best answer. Choice *C* is incorrect because /th/ is an example of a digraph, not a consonant blend.

13. C: *Passes* ends in a continuous sound. A continuous sound is one that can be held and extended, in contrast to stop sounds. Whether a word ends with a continuous or stop sounds affects its pronunciation. Examples of continuous sounds are /s/, /r/, and /z/, while examples of stop sounds are /t/, /d/, and /k/.

14. A: Students' ability to decode words based on their knowledge of morphemes. Morphemes are the smallest units of individual meaning in a language; compound words such as *classroom* and *bookshelf* consist of two morphemes that combine to form a new word. Compound words allow students to apply their existing vocabulary to discover new words. Choice *C* is incorrect because prefixes and suffixes include examples such as *un-, pre-, -tion,* and *-ible,* which are all useful morphemes for decoding language but are not the same as compound words. Choice *D* is incorrect because blending involves combining letter sounds, not words.

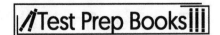

15. C: This is an example of a semantic error, which is sometimes referred to as an error in meaning. In the example, the student replaced *globe* with *world* and *chat* with *talk*. The substitutions fit the context of the sentence and are not incorrect in meaning; in this type of error, the student anticipates the meaning of the sentence and uses the word they expect to see, regardless of whether it actually appears in the sentence. A syntactic miscue (Choice *A*) is one that preserves the grammar of the sentence (for example, reading *the* instead of *a*), while a graphophonemic miscue (Choice *D*) occurs when a student mispronounces a word or replaces it with something that looks similar (for example, *tough* instead of *though*).

16. B: *So* and *sew* are homophones. Homophone literally means "same sound"; homophones are words that are spelled differently but pronounced the same.

17. A: The two types of morphemes are free and bound. Free morphemes are those that can stand alone as words with independent meaning (sometimes referred to as base or root words), while bound morphemes are affixes (prefixes, suffixes, inflectional affixes) that must be attached to a free morpheme to have meaning. For example, in the word *unknown, known* is a free morpheme, and *un-* is a bound morpheme.

18. C: Structural analysis asks students to break a word down into its component parts of free and bound morphemes to decode its meaning. As such, words that contain a root with many affixes are most useful for this approach. *Indestructible* has two affixes, *in-* and *-ble,* attached to the root *destruct,* so it is well suited to this type of analysis.

19. B: *R*-controlled vowels are those that are followed by the letter *r*, transforming the sound (compare the vowel sounds in *cart* and *cat*). Thus, the correct answer is *cart.*

20. C: They are neither long nor short. As in the previous example, compare the sound produced by a short vowel such as in *cat* with the *r*-controlled vowel in *cart,* or the long vowel produced by *care* with the *r*-controlled vowel in *car.*

21. A: *Pop* is a CVC word. CVC refers to the word's spelling—consonant, vowel, consonant. Other common patterns in English include VC, CVCC, and CVVC words, among others.

22. B: The ability to replace one sound with another, often to produce a new word, is called sound substitution.

23. D: The teacher is assessing students' ability to recognize individual words as discrete units of meaning, which is considered word analysis.

24. A: Have the student incorporate physical motion when she reads multisyllabic words, such as clapping or tapping the desk to count syllables. Incorporating physical motion is a useful strategy to help the student become more aware of the individual sounds as she produces them. Choice *B* is not the best answer because it only helps her read the target words but doesn't provide a skill she can use independently. Choice *C* is also not the best answer for an early learner and would be time consuming for decoding everyday text. Choice *D* is also not the best way to provide a practical skill.

Fluency

1. B: Spelling conventions is the area of study that involves mechanics, usage, and sentence formation. Mechanics refers to spelling, punctuation, and capitalization. Usage refers to the use of the various parts

of speech within sentences, and sentence formation is the order in which the various words in a sentence appear. Generally speaking, word analysis is the breaking down of words into morphemes and word units in order to arrive at the word's meaning. Morphemes are the smallest units of a written language that carry meaning, and phonics refers to the study of letter-sound relationships.

2. A: Reading fluency involves how accurately a child reads each individual word within a sentence, the speed at which a child reads, and the expression the child applies while reading. Therefore, accuracy, rate, and prosody are the three key areas of reading fluency.

3. A: If a child can accurately read text with consistent speed and appropriate expression while demonstrating comprehension, the child is said to have reading fluency skills. Without the ability to read fluently, a child's reading comprehension (Choice *C*) will be limited.

4. A: Poems are an effective method for teaching fluency, since rhythmic sounds and rhyming words build a child's understanding of phonemic awareness.

5. A: Syntax refers to the arrangement of words and phrases to form well-developed sentences and paragraphs. Semantics has to do with language meaning. Grammar is a composite of all systems and structures utilized within a language and includes syntax, word morphology, semantics, and phonology. Cohesion and coherence of oral and written language are promoted through a full understanding of syntax, semantics, and grammar.

6. B: Informal reading assessments allow teachers to create differentiated assessments that target reading skills of individual students. In this way, teachers can gain insight into a student's reading strengths and weaknesses. Informal assessments can help teachers decide what content and strategies need to be targeted. However, standardized reading assessments provide all students with the same structure to assess multiple skills at one time. Standardized reading assessments cannot be individualized. Such assessments are best used for gaining an overview of student reading abilities.

7. D: Students within a single classroom come with various background knowledge, interests, and needs. Thus, it's unrealistic to find texts that apply to all. Students benefit when a wide range of fiction and nonfiction texts are available in a variety of genres, promoting differentiated instruction.

8. D: This answer alludes to both read-alouds and think-alouds. Modeling of fluency can be done through read-alouds. Proper pace, phrasing, and expression of text can be modeled when teachers read aloud to their students. During think-alouds, teachers verbalize their thought processes when orally reading a selection. The teacher's explanations may describe strategies they use as they read to monitor their comprehension. In this way, teachers explicitly model the metacognition processes that good readers use to construct meaning from a text.

Vocabulary, Academic Language, and Background Knowledge

1. D: Since the sentence contains two independent clauses and a dependent clause, the sentence is categorized as compound-complex:

> Independent clause: *I accepted the change of seasons*
>
> Independent clause: *I started to appreciate the fall*
>
> Dependent clause: *Although I wished it were summer*

2. B: Since the sentence contains two independent clauses connected by a conjunction, it is referred to as a compound sentence.

Independent clause: *The teacher directed the children's attention to the diagram*

Independent clause: *The children couldn't understand the information*

Conjunction: *But*

3. D: The first sentence is written quite informally and gives a clear impression that the exchange is on a socially-relaxed level. The second sentence is written quite formally and gives a clear impression that the exchange is academic or professional in nature. Although both sentences carry the same message—to respond to the messenger as quickly as possible—the register, or level of formality, is very different.

Accent refers to the way in which certain words are pronounced by an individual and is usually dependent on where a person resides. Dialect refers to how groups of people from a specific geographical region manipulate their language. Point of view refers to a person's interpretation of or feelings toward an event. In literature, a point of view refers to a character's interpretation of or feelings toward an event.

4. A: The three tiers of vocabulary are as follows:

Conversational: informal, more relaxed

Academic: more professional, with vocabulary intended to challenge critical thinking skills

Domain-specific language: a unique vocabulary inventory that focuses around a given discipline or computer language

5. B: Word choice is the trait that teaches the use of precise language. Teachers can enhance this trait in students by helping them to use exact language that is accurate, concise, precise, and lively.

6. D: Intentional writing practice for the purpose of communicating refers to purposeful writing. Students can use this as a method of thinking through issues and solving problems related to writing.

7. C: Speaking, Listening, Reading, and Writing are the four elements of literacy development. As social beings, children begin to recognize that with effective literacy skills, their social, emotional, and physical needs can be met, and their curiosity can be satisfied.

8. C: Synonyms, Antonyms, and Homonyms are examples of semantic relationships. There are five types of semantic relationships, including the three noted in the question. The other two are Hyponyms and Meronyms.

9. B: A utilitarian combination of two or more languages that springs up where different linguistic groups overlap is known as a pidgin; it is used for communication tasks but not as a first language. However, when that pidgin becomes entrenched in the culture and is then taught to children as their first, native language, it is known as a Creole. *C* and *D* are not correct because they both refer to vocabulary, not to entire languages. Jargon is the vocabulary of a specific field or industry, and regionalisms are the vocabulary of a specific place.

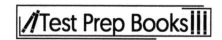

10. A: A dialect of a language refers to one version of that language that follows specific patterns of grammar, spelling, pronunciation, and vocabulary. In this sense, then, Standard English is simply one of many different dialects of English. Standard English is not the original form of English because the language has evolved considerably over the past several centuries and will most likely continue to do so in the future. Also, there is nothing that makes Standard English more complex or grammatical than other dialects of English. Although other dialects may deviate from the grammar used in Standard English, these dialects still follow their own predictable rules and patterns of grammar.

11. A: Slang refers to non-standard expressions that are not used in elevated speech and writing. Slang tends to be specific to one group or time period and is commonly used within groups of young people during their conversations with each other. Jargon refers to the language used in a specialized field. The vernacular is the native language of a local area, and a dialect is one form of a language in a certain region. Thus, Choices *B*, *C*, and *D* are incorrect.

12. D: Colloquial language is that which is used conversationally or informally, in contrast to professional or academic language. While *ain't* is common in conversational English, it is a non-standard expression in academic writing. For college-bound students, high school should introduce them to the expectations of a college classroom, so *B* is not the best answer. Teachers should also avoid placing moral or social value on certain patterns of speech. Rather than teaching students that their familiar speech patterns are bad, teachers should help students learn when and how to use appropriate forms of expression, so Choice *C* is wrong. *Ain't* is in the dictionary, so Choice *A* is incorrect, both in the reason for counseling and in the factual sense.

13. D: The author's word choice that contributes to the style and mood. An author's diction may be elevated, academic, colloquial, melancholy, confessional, or any other mood or way of expression. Discussing a writer's diction requires students to closely consider the types of words used in a text, their denotations and connotations, and the impression they give to the reader.

14. C: Metacognition is another word for "thinking about thinking." By engaging students in this metacognitive activity, the teacher allows students to evaluate their goals, study methods, and strengths and weaknesses, and helps them take responsibility for their own learning process.

15. A: The three most important factors for choosing vocabulary that will contribute the most to students' development are frequency (how often will students encounter this word in their studies?), utility (will students have many chances to use this word in different contexts, or is this word's usage very limited in scope and applicability?), and level of knowledge (is this word already part of students' established vocabulary, or will this word be an opportunity for them to learn something new?).

Comprehension

1. C: Literary analysis of a fictional text involves several areas of study, including character development, setting, and plot. Although points of view refer to a specific area of study in literary analysis, it is only one area. Word analysis does not involve the study of elements within a fictional text.

2. D: Informational texts generally contain five key elements in order to be considered informative. These five elements include the author's purpose, the major ideas, supporting details, visual aids, and key vocabulary. Narratives are accounts—either spoken or written—of an event or a story. Persuasive texts, such as advertisements, use persuasive language to try to convince the reader to act or feel a certain way. Informational texts strive to share factual information about a given subject in order to advance a reader's knowledge.

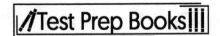

3. A: When a person infers something, he or she is demonstrating the ability to extract key information and make logical assumptions based on that information. The information provided is not direct, but implied. Being able to navigate a variety of texts independently has nothing to do with inference; it demonstrates a student's reading comprehension and fluency. Successfully summarizing and paraphrasing texts are advanced literacy skills that demonstrate a student's reading comprehension and writing proficiency.

4. D: Story maps are a specific type of visual aid that helps younger children develop a clearer understanding of a story being read. Story maps may represent the beginning, middle, and ending of a story, or they may be used to develop a clearer picture of each character's personality and traits, unfold the story's plot, or establish the setting.

5. C: Informational texts organized with headings, subheadings, sidebars, hyperlinks and other features help strengthen the reader's reading comprehension and vocabulary knowledge. A glossary defines terms and words used within a text.

6. C: Third person is a term used to refer to a specific point of view in literature. A third person omniscient point of view develops the point of view of each character within a given story and allows the reader to understand each character's feelings as well as their interpretation of a story's events. Third person limited only offers insight into one character, usually the main character. Character analysis is the intimate study of one character within the story—the character's physical characteristics, personality traits, and relationships to the story's elements and other characters. The story's plot refers to the story's main events; it usually reveals the problem and how it might be resolved. A genre of writing is the specific style of writing the author employs—fiction, nonfiction, mystery, narrative, or informational text.

7. B: Narratives are personal accounts of a time period, event, or an individual, with the purpose of documenting, recording, or sharing such factual information. By contrast, fiction is a genre of writing that is fabricated. Informational texts are academic texts used to further a student's mastery of a given subject, and research papers are written reports students write to demonstrate their understanding of a given area of study that has been researched.

8. C: Pathos refers to the author's appeal to the audience or reader's emotions. Ethos refers to the level of credibility of a piece of writing. Logos refers to the author's appeal to the audience or reader's logic. Kairos refers to the most opportune moment to do something. Therefore, the correct answer is pathos.

9. A: Firsthand accounts are given by primary sources—individuals who provide personal or expert accounts of an event, subject matter, time period, or of an individual. They are viewed more as objective accounts than subjective. Secondary sources are accounts given by an individual or group of individuals who were not physically present at the event or who did not have firsthand knowledge of an individual or time period. Secondary sources are sources that have used research in order to create a written work. Direct and indirect sources are not terms used in literary circles.

10. C: When authors use hyperbole, they are using extreme exaggeration to strongly state a point or evoke a specific emotion in the reader. Idioms can be in the form of words, phrases, or sentences that are expressed figuratively, but they carry a literal meaning that readers must infer. Metaphors are literary devices that compare two unlike entities, as in "The United States is a melting pot." Alliteration is a poetic device that repeats the beginning consonant sound throughout a sentence or phrase strictly for entertainment—"The **b**all **b**ounced along the **b**lue **b**alcony."

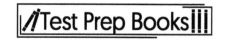
11. D: Flashback is a technique used to give more background information in a story. None of the other concepts are directly related to going back in time.

12. A: Graphic organizers are a method of integrating knowledge and ideas. A graphic organizer can be one of many different visual tools for connecting concepts to help students understand information.

13. D: Four concepts that teach listening skills are focusing, looking, non-verbal cues, and verbal cues. Behaviors that enable good listening skills should not be expected. They need to be taught. Students need to learn the difference between what an excellent listener does and what poor listening behaviors are.

Practice Test #3

Planning, Organizing, and Managing Reading Instruction Based on Ongoing Assessment

1. What types of questions should be offered in an assessment in order to check for its validity?
    a. Open-ended questions only
    b. Selected-response questions
    c. Both open-ended questions and multiple-choice questions
    d. None of these

2. Which is NOT a component of an effective reading lesson?
    a. Presentation
    b. Guided Practice
    c. Modeling
    d. Research

3. If the majority of students in the classroom did not master a skill, what is the next step that a teacher should take?
    a. Reteach the skill to the entire class
    b. Break the class into smaller groups to remediate the skill
    c. Have students mediate with each other about the skill
    d. Move on to the next skill because time is critical

4. What nonfiction texts can be used to teach reading standards?
    I. United States documents
    II. Magazines for pleasure
    III. Science and social studies textbooks
    a. III only
    b. II and III
    c. I and III
    d. I, II, and III

5. When selecting and organizing intervention groups, which of the following is most important?
    a. Organizing students according to their level
    b. Organizing students according to their grades on their prior report cards
    c. Organizing students according to the opinions of the students' previous teachers
    d. Organizing students according to their behavior in the classroom

6. A student has quickly written a story and turned it in without reading it. To help reinforce the POWER strategy, the teacher tells the student go back and read his story. This POWER stage is called what?
    a. Prewriting
    b. Evaluating
    c. Organizing
    d. Revising

7. During which stage of the POWER strategy are graphic organizers used?
    a. Pre-writing
    b. Organizing
    c. Writing
    d. Evaluating

8. A teacher wants his students to write a story over two weeks. They are instructed to write a draft the first day. On each of the following days, he asks the students to develop and edit the story for one of the following: ideas, organization, voice, word choice, sentence fluency, conventions, and presentation. What does this teaching technique incorporate?
    a. Ideas
    b. POWER strategy
    c. Cross-curricular integration
    d. 6+1 Traits

9. Which trait teaches students to build the framework of their writing?
    a. Conventions
    b. Word choice
    c. Ideas
    d. Organization

10. Which trait ultimately forms the content of the writing?
    a. Conventions
    b. Word choice
    c. Ideas
    d. Voice

Word Analysis

1. What is schwa?
    a. The most common vowel sound in spoken English, such as the first vowel in *banana*
    b. The vowel sound produced by two adjacent vowels, such as in the word *bear*
    c. The silent letters that appear in words such as *listen* and *lamb*
    d. The function of consonants as vowels, such as in *sky* and *cow*

2. A teacher shares the following set of words with her students: *cap, pat, sad*. She then asks students what sound they have in common. What skill is she assessing?
    a. Alphabetic principle
    b. Phonetic spelling
    c. Sound identity
    d. Digraph blending

3. Which of the following is an example of a graphophonemic miscue?
    a. A student misreads *faith* as *father*.
    b. A student misreads *improper* as *unproper*.
    c. A student misreads *taken* as *take*.
    d. A student misreads *large* as *big*.

4. What is true of the relationship between graphemes and phonemes?
   a. Each phoneme corresponds to a single grapheme.
   b. Graphemes are combinations of letters that, in turn, produce phonemes.
   c. Graphemes are the letter(s) that represent phonemes.
   d. Phonemes are related to pronunciation, whereas graphemes are not.

5. In a first-grade class, a teacher brings a collection of pictures cut out from newspapers and magazines. Students are instructed to choose a couple of pictures, write sentences or a short story about the pictures, and then share what they've written. One student is reluctant to share his writing, though, because he is worried about his spelling—for example, he has a hard time remembering how to spell *would* and writes *wud* instead. What would be an appropriate response from the teacher?
   a. Assure him that it's fine to try his best to spell a word how he thinks it sounds.
   b. Give him additional practice in phonemic awareness.
   c. Correct all of his spelling on in-class assignments.
   d. Allow him to deliver his story orally rather than in writing.

6. How should teachers approach common words with irregular or uncommon spellings, such as *said* and *goes*?
   a. Let students learn them implicitly through repeated exposure in text.
   b. Teach them as sight words through direct instruction.
   c. Explain the etymology that leads to diverse spelling patterns in English.
   d. Ignore them in favor of high-frequency words with regular spelling patterns.

7. Which of the following is an example of a word that ends with an open syllable?
   a. Speeches
   b. Education
   c. Beginning
   d. Birthday

8. Which of the following is an example of a word family used in building phonemic awareness in readers?
   a. Eat, ate, eaten
   b. Bat, mat, sat
   c. Dog, cat, mouse
   d. Wind, unwind, rewind

9. What best characterizes a student who has mastered letter recognition?
   a. A student is able to recite the alphabet in order.
   b. A student is able to produce both print and cursive letters.
   c. A student is able to recognize upper- and lowercase letters as well as the sounds and names of letters.
   d. A student is able to recognize that a letter is the same even when it produces different sounds in different words.

10. A class is starting to learn consonant digraphs. Which would be the most appropriate ending digraph sound to learn for a beginning reading class?
   a. /sh/ in bush
   b. /gh/ in though
   c. /ey/ in they
   d. /ou/ in you

11. A fourth-grade class is going to take a field trip to an American history museum. Before the trip, students read an informative article about the founding of America and the Revolutionary War. One student volunteers to read aloud to the class, and she reads the words "Constitution" and "Declaration of Independence" with the correct stress and pronunciation. However, after she has finished reading, the teacher asks if she has heard of those documents before, and she says no. Which of the following best explains how she arrived at her correct pronunciation of those words?
   a. Even if she doesn't know exactly what they mean, she has probably encountered them in print before and was able to make a close guess as to their meaning and pronunciation.
   b. She knew how to pronounce the base words, *constitute* and *declare,* and applied that knowledge to pronouncing their derived forms.
   c. The class has read several other history-related texts before, so she already had practice pronouncing academic vocabulary from that subject.
   d. She recognized the orthographic pattern *-tion* and understood that words with that ending place stress on the penultimate syllable.

12. Which of the following is NOT true of phonemic awareness in relation to reading development?
   a. It refers to the awareness that spoken phonemes are also the sounds that make up written words.
   b. Phonemic awareness develops after students have learned basic spelling concepts.
   c. Phonemic awareness is more highly correlated to success in learning to read than general intelligence or listening comprehension.
   d. Strong phonemic awareness can improve reading comprehension.

13. As part of encouraging a language-rich environment, which of the following best describes the foundation of a wide-reading policy?
   a. A range of texts are chosen by the teacher and provided in class.
   b. Students have access to self-selected texts they can take home.
   c. Books focus on grade-level topics pulled from a variety of subjects.
   d. Students learn the importance of reading novels and literary texts.

14. A teacher reads to her kindergarten class from a patterned book:
   > The fish is blue.
   > The dog is white.
   > The fish swims.
   > The dog runs.

As she reads, she holds the book so it is facing the class, points to the words as she reads, and stops on each page to ask students questions about the story. What is true of patterned books for this level of readers?
   a. They should only include words from students' spoken vocabulary.
   b. They should only include sound-letter relationships students have learned.
   c. Teachers should constantly change the books they read to students, avoiding repetition.
   d. Teachers should choose books without many pictures so students can focus on the words.

15. What is the Matthew effect?
   a. The effect of culture shock
   b. The effect of accumulated advantage
   c. The effect of language immersion
   d. The effect of social learning

16. How is a Yopp-Singer test conducted?
   a. The student reads aloud a list of twenty-two words. The teacher then evaluates the student's ability to distinguish long and short vowel sounds.
   b. The teacher reads a list of twenty-two words, and the student writes down the words that are spoken. The teacher then evaluates the student's conventional spelling skills.
   c. The student reads aloud a list of twenty-two words. The teacher then evaluates the student's phoneme blending skills.
   d. The teacher reads a list of twenty-two words, and the student provides the individual sounds of each word in order. The teacher then evaluates the student's phoneme segmentation skills.

17. A teacher is about to start a unit that introduces several new sound blends. He has created an assessment for the end of the unit in which he will spend about five minutes one-on-one having students read from a list of target words and evaluating their performance. What else would be the most helpful to add to his assessment plan?
   a. An informal group assessment after the formal individual assessment
   b. A written evaluation after the oral assessment
   c. A self-assessment for students to complete after the unit
   d. A one-on-one pretest at the beginning of the unit to compare results

18. What describes students' understanding that text is read from left to right and top to bottom?
   a. Syntactic awareness
   b. Directionality
   c. Word segmentation
   d. Print production

19. Which of the following best describes the Language Experience Approach (LEA)?
   a. A teacher selects texts that correspond with students' cultural backgrounds.
   b. When a teacher reads a story or new words, students stand up and complete physical responses to the text and vocabulary.
   c. Students share a memorable personal experience with the teacher, who writes down the experience. Students and the teacher then read the dictated text together.
   d. The classroom contains many instances of everyday language, such as signs, posters, and word labels on objects around the room.

20. During independent writing, a student writes long run-on sentences with no clear way to distinguish where one sentence ends and the next begins. What skill would be most useful for the teacher to focus on with this student?
   a. Explain how the lines and margins work on a piece of paper.
   b. Practice word awareness with her, such as counting the words in a sentence.
   c. Show her how sentences end with a period and start with an uppercase letter.
   d. Give her a worksheet to practice uppercase and lowercase letters.

21. What is etymology?
    a. Study of word origins
    b. Spelling conventions
    c. Study of regional pronunciations
    d. Natural patterns of intonation

22. A teacher wants to incorporate a lesson on poetry to help students practice concepts of rhyme, rhythm, and diction. Which of the following would be a useful poetry form to emphasize syllable count?
    a. Open form
    b. Haiku
    c. Stream of consciousness
    d. Couplet

23. What is a semantic map?
    a. A visual representation of related words that activates students' background knowledge and helps with schema building
    b. A way for students to break down words into their component meanings when decoding new vocabulary
    c. A method of analyzing a word's grammatical function within a sentence
    d. A visualization of words a student already knows, maybe knows, and doesn't know but wants to learn

24. Which of the following is true of syntactic instruction for English Language Learners?
    a. It is not as important as instruction in semantics or pronunciation.
    b. Students generally have a strong background in grammar because other countries teach grammar more frequently than America does.
    c. Students need direct teaching of word order in English, which may be different from their first language.
    d. It should focus on spelling and writing skills, since students' first language may not use the same writing system.

Fluency

1. Reading fluency is best described as the ability to do what?
    a. Read smoothly and accurately
    b. Comprehend what is read
    c. Demonstrate phonetic awareness
    d. Properly pronounce a list of words

2. A teacher is in the midst of creating a unit in which he hopes to further promote students' reading skills. In this process, the teacher should make sure that:
    a. Vocabulary development is central to all activities within the unit.
    b. Data from student reading assessments is used to target reading skills that reflect the students' needs.
    c. Students are required to use words provided on a word wall within multiple writing assignments.
    d. Instruction is the same for all students.

3. A teacher needs to assess students' accuracy in reading grade-appropriate, high frequency, and irregular sight words. Which of the following strategies would be most appropriate for this purpose?

    a. The teacher gives students a list of words to study for a spelling test that will be administered the following week.

    b. The teacher allows each student to bring their favorite book from home and has each student read their selected text aloud independently.

    c. The teacher administers the Stanford Structural Analysis assessment to determine students' rote memory and application of morphemes contained within the words.

    d. The teacher records how many words each student reads correctly when reading aloud a list of a teacher-selected, grade-appropriate words.

4. Which of the following is true of first language acquisition?

    a. Children need some instruction from parents or caregivers to learn a first language.

    b. Children first begin forming complete words when they are about two years old.

    c. Children experiment with the sounds of a language before they form words.

    d. Children have no language comprehension before they can speak.

5. Which of the following is true of second language acquisition?

    a. Students learn best through memorization of new vocabulary words.

    b. Second language acquisition follows the same stages as first language acquisition.

    c. Advanced fluency is achieved when the speaker has no accent in his or her second language.

    d. Second language learners experience a preproduction stage, during which they are unable to produce verbal expressions.

6. Which of the following would NOT be a recommended vocabulary teaching strategy?

    a. Focusing on specialized academic jargon that students will encounter in college

    b. Creating a word map to understand the connection between vocabulary terms

    c. Accessing prior knowledge when introducing a new area of vocabulary

    d. Providing examples of how to use terms inside and outside of class

7. Which of the following is an example of incidental learning in vocabulary development?

    a. After reading a story in class, the teacher provides students with a list of keywords to know from the text.

    b. While reading a novel for class, a student encounters an unfamiliar word and looks it up in the dictionary.

    c. As part of a writing assignment, students are instructed to utilize certain academic words and expressions in their essays.

    d. After getting back the results of a vocabulary exam, students are assigned to make personal study guides based on the words that they missed on the test.

8. A teacher is considering integrating some media sources like television and the Internet into his classroom, but he is unsure of how effective it will be. Which of the following is true about media literacy in language development?

a. Instruction should focus only on professional media sources such as scientific journals and mainstream news publications to emphasize Standard English skills.

b. In the twenty-first century, every student has access to and proficiency in using the Internet, so it is unnecessary to spend time on building skills in class.

c. Students should explore media resources in their personal areas of interest to develop regular language habits in an enjoyable way.

d. The Internet serves as a huge distraction for students and should not be part of instruction.

Vocabulary, Academic Language, and Background Knowledge

1. In vocabulary instruction for English Language Learners, what is a disadvantage of relying on cognates?

a. Students can get confused with false cognates, hindering comprehension.

b. Students will lose motivation to study English because they will find it too easy.

c. Not every language has the same number of cognates in English, so it creates an unfair advantage for students who speak closely related languages.

d. Most cognates are related to conversational words, not academic vocabulary.

2. A fourth-grade class is reading a short story about a girl who starts a Victory Garden during World War II. The teacher decides to include an accompanying informational text about rationing and other home-front efforts during the war. When selecting an appropriate reading level for the informational text, the teacher should select something that does which of the following?

a. Matches students' frustration reading level.

b. Matches students' independent reading level.

c. Matches students' instructional reading level.

d. Matches students' comprehension reading level.

3. A seventh-grade teacher introduces a week-long unit on rain forest conservation, and she begins the lesson by having students start a KWL chart on the board. Why did she include this activity?

a. She wants to motivate students by having them engage in a competitive game.

b. She wants to activate students' background knowledge on the subject.

c. She wants to figure out which students are most interested in the topic.

d. She wants to have students practice formal writing responses.

4. A student is struggling with multiple-choice questions related to academic reading passages. When his teacher asks him to summarize the contents of the passage, he is able to identify and explain the main ideas. Also, his short-answer responses are generally high scoring. How can his teacher help him improve his overall test scores?

a. Give him additional vocabulary homework focused on high-frequency academic words.

b. Give him additional time to complete practice tests.

c. Give him additional background reading about grade-level-appropriate academic topics.

d. Give him additional practice in identifying and responding to different question types.

5. A teacher prepared a list of need-to-know academic vocabulary words for students to master by the end of the semester, including words such as *analyze, observation,* and *hypothesize*. Which tier of vocabulary best describes these words?
    a. Tier 1
    b. Tier 2
    c. Tier 3
    d. Tier 4

6. In academic reading contexts, what is an advantage of building students' sight word vocabulary?
    a. The future academic texts that students will encounter during their education will primarily consist of sight words.
    b. Students will not have to stop and decode every word and can instead improve their reading rate and focus on overall textual comprehension.
    c. Most sight words form the roots of academic vocabulary, so students will be able to infer the meanings of unfamiliar words.
    d. Sight words contain all forty-four phonemes found in English, which can aid with academic vocabulary pronunciation.

7. A teacher wants students to learn academic vocabulary related to the root *cred*. Which of the following is an example of vocabulary instruction through reciprocal teaching?
    a. Students identify instances of words using *cred* in their daily reading and homework assignments during the week and write the words in a personal vocabulary log.
    b. Students are given a list of relevant words, such as *credible, discredit*, and *credulity*, and the teacher explains the meanings and usage of each.
    c. Students are given a list of relevant words and must write ten practice sentences using the words in context.
    d. Students are given several examples of *cred* before brainstorming other examples together and are then put in pairs and assigned one new *cred* word to introduce to the class.

8. Which of the following is an example of a pair of synonyms?
    a. Click, trick
    b. Happy, joyful
    c. Excited, disappointed
    d. Philosophy, sophisticated

9. A teacher wants to introduce a Word of the Day as part of classroom language enrichment. Which of the following is the most useful way to incorporate the project into class?
    a. She should not start a Word of the Day because research shows that students have low retention of daily vocabulary and are not able to fully learn more than three new vocabulary words per week.
    b. She should make a poster on the wall with the Word of the Day, add one word to it every day, and then take it down and change it at the end of the week.
    c. She should introduce the word through explicit instruction and then give students a chance to read and write the word in context.
    d. She should give students a weekly quiz in which they have to match words and definitions.

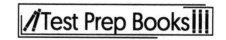

10. Students are assigned to read the following passage: "In the king's court, flattery was the surest path to success. The most powerful courtier was also the most obsequious." The teacher asks his students to use context clues to come up with a general definition for *obsequious*. Which of the following best describes how to use context clues in this situation?
    a. The students should refer to a glossary or a footnote in the text that provides explanations for specific terms.
    b. The students should consider the part of speech and the words closely surrounding the unknown term.
    c. The students should get in small groups to share their ideas about the definition of the term.
    d. The students should recall their previous knowledge of historical texts.

11. Which of the following is the most helpful for guiding classroom dictionary usages?
    a. Students should have limited access to dictionaries because they should be able to decode most new vocabulary using other skills, such as word analysis and context clues.
    b. ELs should be able to access dictionaries during in-class writing, but they are generally not necessary for native English speakers.
    c. Students should learn that the first dictionary definition is always the most commonly used one.
    d. Students should learn to recognize the different information contained within a dictionary entry, such as spelling, pronunciation, multiple definitions, and word origins.

12. A teacher gives students a list of vocabulary words pulled from a poetry unit and asks them to identify how comfortable they are using each word. Which category would be appropriate to describe words that a student has encountered before but is not fully confident using yet?
    a. Unknown words
    b. Acquainted words
    c. Auditory words
    d. Established words

13. Which of the following is true of about instruction in an English classroom?
    a. In English class, instruction should emphasize reading and writing.
    b. Teachers should place students in small groups with other students with similar learning styles and allow for differentiated instruction that focuses on their language strengths.
    c. Kinesthetic and tactile lessons are important for early learners, while older students can focus almost exclusively on written texts.
    d. Students should be immersed in a language-rich environment where they can explore new words through reading, writing, listening, and speaking.

14. Which of the following best describes schema building?
    a. Developing clusters of related knowledge
    b. Basing academic learning on real-life experiences
    c. Employing learning strategies to monitor progress
    d. Creating visual aids to translate written words into new mediums

15. Students have been learning how to use different reference texts in completing academic assignments. While working on a persuasive essay about a social problem facing modern teens, a student notices that he has used the term problem repeatedly in his writing and wants to find a way to vary his word choice. What would be the best reference text to locate possible alternative words?
   a. Dictionary
   b. Thesaurus
   c. Encyclopedia
   d. Glossary

Comprehension

1. Which of the following can be useful when working with intervention groups of struggling readers?
   a. Having the teacher read aloud a text to the students while they take notes
   b. Having students read the text silently
   c. Giving independent work and explaining the direction in details before the students take it back to their seat
   d. Providing games for them to play while the teacher observes

2. What should be taught and mastered first when teaching reading comprehension?
   a. Theme
   b. Word analysis and fluency
   c. Text evidence
   d. Writing

3. What is the method of categorizing text by its structure and literary elements called?
   a. Fiction
   b. Nonfiction
   c. Genre
   d. Plot

4. A reader is distracted from following a story because she is having trouble understanding why a character has decided to cut school, so the reader jumps to the next page to find out where the character is headed. This is an example of what?
   a. Self-monitoring comprehension
   b. KWL charts
   c. Metacognitive skills
   d. Directed reading-thinking activities

5. A class silently reads a passage on the American Revolution. Once they are done, the teacher asks who were the two sides fighting, why were they fighting, and who won. What skill is the teacher gauging?
   a. Orthographic development
   b. Fluency
   c. Comprehension
   d. Phonics

6. Which trait is most commonly associated with giving individuality and style to writing?
   a. Voice
   b. Word choice
   c. Presentation
   d. Ideas

7. Which mode of writing aims to inform the reader objectively about a particular subject or idea and typically contains definitions, instructions, or facts within its subject matter?
   a. Argumentative
   b. Informative
   c. Narrative
   d. Descriptive

8. Editorials, letters of recommendation, and cover letters most likely incorporate which writing mode?
   a. Argumentative
   b. Informative
   c. Narrative
   d. Descriptive

9. The type of writing mode an author chooses to use is dependent on which of the following elements?
   I. The audience
   II. The primary purpose
   III. The main idea
   a. III only
   b. I and II
   c. I and III
   d. I, II, and III

10. Which of the following refers to what an author wants to express about a given subject?
    a. Primary purpose
    b. Plot
    c. Main idea
    d. Characterization

11. Which organizational style is used in the following passage?
    There are several reasons why the new student café has not been as successful as expected. One factor is that prices are higher than originally advertised, so many students cannot afford to buy food and beverages there. Also, the café closes rather early; as a result, students go out in town to other late-night gathering places rather than meeting friends at the café on campus.

    a. Cause and effect order
    b. Compare and contrast order
    c. Spatial order
    d. Time order

12. Short, succinct sentences are best written for which of the following audiences?
    a. Adults or people more familiar with a subject
    b. Children or people less familiar a subject
    c. Politicians and academics
    d. University students

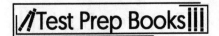

13. Which of the following defines the stage of writing that involves adding to, removing, rearranging, or re-writing sections of a piece?
    a. The revising stage
    b. The publishing stage
    c. The writing stage
    d. The pre-writing stage

Answer Explanations for Practice Test #3

Planning, Organizing, and Managing Reading Instruction Based on Ongoing Assessment

1. C: In order to check assessments for validity, it's important to understand what both question types entail for students. Selected-response questions cover a broad range of topics in a shorter period of time. However, students can guess the correct response on selected-response questions. For example, a typical multiple-choice question provides four answers from which a student can choose. This gives students a 25 percent chance of guessing the correct answer. Therefore, the results of select-response assessments are not always valid. Open-ended questions are longer and more time-consuming. However, these questions assess students' skill levels more effectively. Open-ended assessments also allow students to use text-based evidence to support their answers.

2. D: Research is not a component of planning an effective reading lesson according to the California state standards. California state standards state that an effective reading lesson consists of presentations, direct instruction, guided practice, modeling, and intervention. Although a teacher may need to conduct research to provide a rich experience for their lesson, research is not a component of reading instruction according to the California state standards.

3. A: If the majority of the class did not master a skill taught, then the best plan is to reteach the skill to the entire class again. To break the class into intervention groups would not be the best use of time. Also, if too many students did not understand the skill, then perhaps the skill was not properly taught the first time. A different teaching approach may be necessary. The utilization of different types of media, more direct instruction, and modeling of the skill should be done several more times before the students are assessed on the skill a second time.

4. C: Good reading strategies are essential for all subject areas across the curriculum. In order to excel in science and social studies, there needs to be a good reading foundation—especially in nonfiction text. The United States documents or science and social studies textbooks may all be used to teach nonfiction. Informational magazines may have good nonfictional material, but these need to be selected carefully, to ensure that the reading is appropriately substantive. Basal readers are also good examples of nonfiction text.

5. A: Intervention groups should be organized based on student performance. Although the behavior of students may be taken into consideration, the organization of group members should be primarily based on each student's performance levels.

6. B: Students should carefully read what they've written during the Evaluating stage of the POWER strategy.

7. B: Graphic organizers are used during the Organizing stage of the POWER strategy. They help students to examine, analyze, and summarize selections they have read and can be used individually or collaboratively in the classroom. Graphic organizers may be sequencing charts, graphs, Venn diagrams, timelines, chain of events organizers, story maps, concept maps, mind maps, webs, outlines, or other visual tools for connecting concepts to achieve understanding.

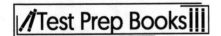

8. D: 6+1 Traits is a model for teaching writing that uses common language to explain writing standards. The 6+1 Traits are the characteristics that make writing readable and effective no matter what genre of writing is being used. These seven traits are ideas, organization, voice, word choice, sentence fluency, conventions, and presentation.

9. D: Organization is the trait that teaches students how to build the framework of their writing. Students choose an organizational strategy or purpose for the writing and build the details upon that structure. There are many purposes for writing, and they all have different frameworks.

10. C: Ideas ultimately form the content of the writing. The Ideas Trait is one of the 6+1 Traits model; it is where students learn to select an important topic for their writing. They are taught to narrow down and focus their idea before further developing it.

Word Analysis

1. A: *Schwa* is the most common vowel sound in spoken English, such as the first vowel in *banana*. Although *schwa* does not appear in written English, it is the most commonly produced sound in spoken English. It sounds something like *uh* and is generally heard in unstressed syllables, such as the first and last syllables in the word *banana;* only the middle, stressed syllable produces a clear *a* sound.

2. C: Sound identity refers to the ability to recognize and identify sounds in context.

3. A: Graphophonemic errors are those in which the student misreads the word as something with a similar sound and spelling, such as if a student misreads *faith* as *father*. Choices *B* and *C* are examples of syntactic errors (words with similar grammatical functions), while Choice *D* is an example of a semantic error (words with similar meanings).

4. C: Graphemes are the letter(s) that represent phonemes. Phonemes are spoken, while graphemes are written. Graphemes are the letters in the alphabet, but some graphemes may correspond with more than one morpheme (such as the letter *c,* which may produce the /s/ or /k/ sound) and vice versa (the /k/ sound may be represented by the letter *c, k,* or *ck*). Also, a grapheme may be a single letter or more than one letter.

5. A: The best strategy would be to assure him that it's fine to try his best to spell a word how he thinks it sounds. At this stage of spelling, it is expected that students will make errors as they refine their phonological and orthographic skills. Choice *B* is not the best answer because, in fact, the spelling *wud* shows clear phonemic awareness; *would* is an example of a word with uncommon spelling, and *wud* is a logical guess at phonetic spelling. Choice *C* is also not correct because, while formal spelling assessment is important, it does not have to overtake informal in-class assignments. Choice *D* is also incorrect because it does not provide the opportunities for writing practice.

6. B: Teach them as sight words through direct instruction. Students should learn to recognize these common words so they can read them with fluency. Because their spellings do not follow common orthographic rules, it is better for teachers to introduce them through explicit teaching rather than wait for students to learn them implicitly (Choice *A*). Choice *C* is not the best approach for beginner learners, and Choice *D* is also incorrect because some of the most useful high-frequency words are those with irregular spellings.

7. D: *Birthday* ends with an open syllable. An open syllable is one that ends with a vowel sound, while a closed syllable ends with a consonant sound.

8. B: Word families used in building phonemic awareness are those that have the same rime and different onsets. Therefore, *bat, mat, sat* is the correct set.

9. C: A student is able to recognize upper- and lowercase letters as well as the sounds and names of letters. Letter recognition includes not only being able to recite the alphabet but also being able to identify the sounds and the names of letters. Students should also be able to recognize both upper- and lowercase letters in context and in isolation.

10. A: The most appropriate ending digraph sound to learn for a beginning reading class is /sh/ in *bush*. When introducing blends and digraphs, teachers should begin with the most common letter combinations that appear in English. /sh/ is a digraph students will encounter much more often than the other answer choices.

11. D: She recognized the orthographic pattern *-tion* and understood that words with that ending place stress on the penultimate syllable. When students are able to correctly pronounce multisyllabic words the first time they encounter them, they are relying on their (conscious or unconscious) awareness of syllabication patterns. Choice *A* is not the best answer because simply recognizing a word visually does not always correlate with being able to pronounce it. Choice *B* is also incorrect because, in this case, the affix *-tion* affects the pronunciation of the base words, so simply recognizing those does not account for placing the correct stress in the derived forms. Choice *C* is also not the best answer because, while background knowledge can contribute to vocabulary awareness, it is not the strongest factor in pronunciation knowledge.

12. B: Phonemic awareness develops after students have learned basic spelling concepts. Students' spelling skills develop in tandem with their phonemic skills; the earliest spelling concepts are often phonetic. Before they can begin to spell and write words, students must first understand that written sounds correspond to spoken phonemes.

13. B: Students have access to self-selected texts they can take home. Wide reading means students are encouraged to read a variety of texts in class, at home, and anywhere else; about academic and nonacademic subjects; about things selected by the teacher and self-selected by the student; in the form of novels, magazines, comic books, or any other text that interests the students. Because students may not have access to reading materials at home, teachers should make sure they have access to reading materials they can take home, such as library books they can check out.

14. A: They should only include words from students' spoken vocabulary. Although students may not be able to read or recognize every word in print, they should be familiar with all of the words in the text because they should come from their spoken vocabulary. Choice *B* is not correct because the book may include sound-letter relationships that haven't been explicitly taught yet (for example, the *wh* in *white* is not a letter combination many earlier readers will have learned). Choice *C* is also not the best answer because, while it is good to present students with a variety of texts, repetition is also useful to help students become familiar with certain stories and sentence patterns. Choice *D* is also not the best answer because pictures can be a useful aid to establishing meaning.

15. B: When applied to reading comprehension and language awareness, the Matthew effect means that students who are exposed to more language earlier in life and who master reading skills are more likely to use those skills to achieve other levels of academic success later in their studies, whereas students who do not build strong reading skills in early grades are likely to struggle more as they move

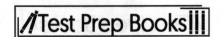

through school. In short, early advantages are likely to lead to greater advantages later on, while early disadvantages are likely to lead to greater disadvantages.

16. D: The teacher reads a list of twenty-two words, and the student provides the individual sounds of each word in order. The teacher then evaluates the student's phoneme segmentation skills.

17. D: A one-on-one pretest at the beginning of the unit to compare results.

18. B: Directionality helps students follow the progression of the text in a book and helps them correctly direct their words in writing.

19. C: Students share a memorable personal experience with the teacher, who writes down the experience. Students and the teacher then read the dictated text together. LEA involves students in the writing and reading process and produces texts based on their real experiences. LEA can be useful after a shared class activity, such as going on a field trip.

20. C: Show her how sentences end with a period and start with an uppercase letter. While the student can most likely speak in complete sentences, she has not learned how to represent them on paper. She still needs explicit instructions in the written signals that one sentence has ended (punctuation) and a new one has started (capitalization). Choice *A* is not the best answer because her problem is run-on sentences, not word tracking or directionality. Choice *B* is also not the best answer because she is having difficulty separating sentences, not words. Finally, Choice *D* is not the best answer because, while distinguishing upper- and lowercase letters is important in this skill, it is not useful if she practices them out of context.

21. A: Etymology, the study of word origins, can help students understand a word's history and development, such as what language it originated from, what root(s) it contains, and how it is related to other vocabulary words.

22. B: Haiku is a very structured form of poetry with specific syllable counts for each line, so it is very appropriate for this kind of lesson. Open form poetry (Choice *A*) is that without regular rhyme or rhythm, so it will not help students with syllable awareness. Stream of consciousness (Choice *C*) is more often found in prose text and is also largely without formal structure. While couplets (Choice *D*) generally have matching syllable patterns, the emphasis is more on the ending rhyme of each line, so it is not as useful as haiku for this exercise.

23. A: A semantic map is a visual representation of related words that activates students' background knowledge and helps with schema building. An example of a semantic map might be writing a target word in the middle of the board inside a large circle and then having other smaller circles branching off with related words (synonyms, antonyms, words with common roots or related to the same topic, etc.). It helps students to organize new knowledge and connect information they already know.

24. C: Students need direct teaching of word order in English, which may be different from their first language. English generally uses subject-verb-object (SVO) word order in sentence structure, while other languages may use SOV or other structures that are not common in English. Students need explicit instruction to recognize the differences and become familiar with the patterns of English sentences. Choice *A* is not the best answer because ELLs need instruction in all of these areas. Choice *B* is also not the best answer because, although some students may have a higher understanding of English grammar than speaking, this is definitely not true of all students and especially not early learners who have not attended school in their native language. Finally, Choice *D* is not the best answer because syntactic

instruction is related to grammar, word order, and sentence structure, which are not the key skills reflected here.

Fluency

1. A: Reading fluency is the ability to accurately read at a socially acceptable pace and with proper expression. Phonetic awareness leads to the proper pronunciation of words and fluency. Once students are able to read fluently, concentration is no longer dedicated toward the process of reading. Instead, students can concentrate on the meaning of a text. Thus, in the developmental process of reading, comprehension follows fluency.

2. B: Strand 11(c) of Competency 11 in the RICA's Content Specifications states the expectation that teachers "(demonstrate the) ability to use the results of assessments to plan effective instruction and interventions . . . and adjust instruction and interventions to meet the identified needs of students."

3. D: Accuracy is measured via the percentage of words that are read correctly with in a given text. Word-reading accuracy is often measured by counting the number of errors that occur per 100 words of oral reading. This information is used to select the appropriate level of text for an individual.

4. C: In the babbling stage, children repeat simple syllables that will later form the building blocks of their first words, such as *ma-ma* and *da-da*. Choice *A* is not correct because children learn their first language simply by being exposed to it, without any formal instruction required. Choice *B* is also incorrect because most children utter their first word by about one year old. Babies demonstrate understanding of language before they are able to actually form words themselves, so Choice *D* is not correct.

5. D: This is the first stage of L2 acquisition, before the learner is ready to communicate in the target language. Both L1 and L2 acquisition clearly follow different stages, so Choice *B* is incorrect. The final stage of L2 development—advanced fluency—does not require the speaker to have a native accent; rather, it refers to the stage at which the speaker encounters no difficulty in expression or comprehension in both conversational and academic settings; thus, Choice *C* is incorrect. L2 learners benefit from a variety of instruction techniques, and students require both input (such as studying new vocabulary words) and output (actually using those words in productive language tasks) in order to develop new skills; therefore, Choice *A* is also incorrect.

6. A: Although it is useful to introduce students to concepts they might encounter in a college classroom, making jargon the focus of instruction at the expense of vocabulary with more widely-applicable usage will not meet the needs of the majority of students in class. The other strategies are all appropriate ways to have students integrate new vocabulary into their existing knowledge structures and their everyday lives.

7. B: Incidental learning contrasts with direct instruction, wherein instructors direct students in the precise meaning of new vocabulary or call students' attention to important vocabulary skills in a given lesson. In incidental learning, students learn new vocabulary as they encounter unfamiliar terms during other learning tasks. In this case, Choice *B* is the correct answer because the student uses a reading assignment as an opportunity to learn a new word. In all of the other answer choices, the instructor is the one guiding the students' attention towards specific vocabulary words.

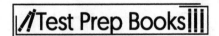

8. C: Students should explore media resources in their personal areas of interest to develop regular language habits in an enjoyable way. Multimedia resources are a powerful educational resource and should be integrated into class instruction when possible, making Choice *D* a poor answer choice. Choice *B* is incorrect because it cannot be assumed that every student has regular access to the internet, and even students who do have home internet access may still need guidance in how to use it to find learning resources. Choice *A* is incorrect because though it is useful to introduce students to academic and professional media sources, the diversity of media available means that these do not need to be the sole emphasis of instruction. Rather, it can be useful to help students explore areas of their own interest and build skills in how to apply language development concepts—e.g., reading comprehension skills, using context to learn new words, keeping a journal of new words and expressions, or formulating a reading response—both inside and outside of the classroom.

Vocabulary, Academic Language, and Background Knowledge

1. A: Students can get confused with false cognates, hindering comprehension. In language learning, cognates are words in the target language that are similar to words in the student's native language. Particularly for students whose native language shares common roots with English, cognates can aid in learning new vocabulary. However, students may encounter false cognates, or English words that look similar to words in their native language but have different meanings. Choice *D,* in particular, is incorrect because, especially with Latin-based languages, cognates often include academic English vocabulary from Latin roots.

2. C: In selecting academic and content-based texts, teachers should target students' instructional reading level, or the level at which they can understand the text with a small amount of guidance from the teacher; their accuracy level should be between 90 and 94 percent. Frustration reading level (Choice A) refers to the level at which students struggle with the text, have a low level of accuracy and comprehension, and become discouraged about reading. Independent reading level (Choice B) refers to the level at which students can read without any assistance; generally, their accuracy level is 95 percent or higher. Instructional reading level is low enough to still challenge students but high enough that students can comfortably follow the material.

3. B: She wants to activate students' background knowledge on the subject. A KWL chart stands for *know—want to know—learned* and allows students to assess their knowledge before, during, and after a lesson. Beginning a lesson with a KWL chart (the "know" and "want to know" sections) allows students to activate their background knowledge, including key vocabulary and concepts. It is also a way for students to predict and anticipate the text's content. Choice *A* is incorrect because this is an example of a collaborative activity, not a competitive one. Choice *C* is also not the best answer because she is trying to engage every student's interest. Finally, Choice *D* is incorrect because a KWL chart is an informal way for students to explore their ideas about a topic.

4. D: His teacher can give him additional practice in identifying and responding to different question types. Because the student is able to summarize the contents and respond to short-answer questions, it is apparent that he is not struggling with comprehending the text or the topic, so Choices *A* and *C* are not the best answers. Rather, he is likely struggling with decoding the different types of academic question forms, such as literal, inferential, and evaluative questions. By building his skills in identifying different question types and patterns, he will be able to more quickly understand what the question is asking and how to locate the information in the text (or whether the question requires him to make an inference not stated in the text, for instance).

5. B: Vocabulary words can generally be divided into Tier 1, Tier 2, and Tier 3. Tier 1 words include high-frequency or sight words, the most basic vocabulary for understanding English. Tier 2 words are more academic words (such as the ones in this example), but they appear across multiple contexts and are not restricted to a single discipline. Finally, Tier 3 words are highly specialized vocabulary related to a single subject (for example, scientific terminology). Tier 4 vocabulary does not exist.

6. B: Students will not have to stop and decode every word and can instead improve their reading rate and focus on overall textual comprehension. Having a strong foundation in sight words (function and high-frequency words) allows students to read those words automatically and instead focus on key content words and decoding any new vocabulary. Choice *A* is incorrect because, as students progress to higher levels of study, texts will contain fewer sight words and more complex terminology. Choice *C* is also incorrect because many academic words are based on Greek or Latin roots, not on sight words. Choice *D* is similarly incorrect; sight words do not prepare students for all the pronunciations they will encounter in developing their academic vocabulary.

7. D: Students are given several examples of *cred* before brainstorming other examples together and are then put in pairs and assigned one new *cred* word to introduce to the class. Reciprocal teaching is based on the gradual release of responsibility model, whereby the teacher introduces a new concept to the class and then gives students the chance to independently engage with the material by making predictions, generating questions, clarifying the content, and summarizing what they have learned.

8. B: Synonyms are words whose meanings are the same or similar, such as *happy* and *joyful*. Choice *A* is an example of words that rhyme, Choice *C* is an example of antonyms (words with opposite meanings), and Choice *D* is an example of words with shared roots.

9. C: She should introduce the word through explicit instruction and then give students a chance to read and write the word in context. The most effective vocabulary instruction occurs when words are not introduced in isolation, as in Choice *D*, but when students are given an opportunity to encounter and use words in both classroom and everyday context. Choice *A* is incorrect; studies show that most students can effectively learn up to nine new vocabulary words per week. Choice *B* is also not the best answer because, while it is useful to keep the Word of the Day on the board or on the wall, words should also be reinforced in subsequent lessons that allow students to use what they have learned.

10. B: The students should consider the part of speech and the words closely surrounding the unknown term. Context clues allow readers to guess the meaning of an unfamiliar word by considering the role it plays in a sentence based on semantic and syntactic clues. For example, students can tell that *obsequious* is being used as an adjective, so it is a word that describes a courtier. They can also use the meaning of earlier words they know—in this case, the first sentence's reference to flattery—to guess that an obsequious person is good at flattering others. Choice *A* is not the best answer because context clues are based on information already in the text, not supplementary references. Choice *C* is also not the best answer for a similar reason; context should be based on the text rather than information from other students. Choice *D* is incorrect because prior knowledge is not involved in context clues either.

11. D: Students should learn to recognize the different information contained within a dictionary entry, such as spelling, pronunciation, multiple definitions, and word origins. Dictionaries have a variety of usages beyond just checking spelling. Teachers should explain the different parts of a dictionary entry and allow students to explore things like how to select the most appropriate definition or how the part of speech affects meaning. Choice *A* is not the best answer because, while those are useful decoding skills, students still need to know how and when to access reference materials. Choice *B* is not correct

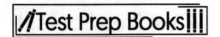

because dictionary skills are relevant for both English Language Learners and native speakers. Finally, Choice *C* is not the best answer; although it is correct, it overlooks many situations in which students may have to choose between more than just the first definition.

12. B: Acquainted words are words that a student has encountered before but is not fully confident using yet. Unknown words (Choice *A*) are those a student has never encountered before; acquainted words are those that are familiar but have not entered regular use in the student's vocabulary; and established words (Choice *D*) are those the student can comfortably use and understand in various contexts.

13. D: Students should be immersed in a language-rich environment where they can explore new words through reading, writing, listening, and speaking. Students should be exposed to language in as many forms as possible to build both academic and real-life language skills. Choices *A* and *C* are not the best answers because speaking and listening are both important aspects of language development in students of all ages. Choice *B* is not the best answer because, while differentiated learning can be helpful, students still need instruction in other modes to continue to develop skills in their weaker areas.

14. A: Developing clusters of related knowledge can be described as schema building. A schema is a mental framework for organizing information; by associating related knowledge, students can keep track of new concepts and vocabulary. Schema-building activities include using titles and headings for related topics and creating word maps for related vocabulary.

15. B: A thesaurus contains synonyms and antonyms, which is what the student is looking for to vary his word choice in the writing assignment.

Comprehension

1. A: Small intervention groups can benefit from a teacher reading a text or small book aloud while students listen and take notes. This helps struggling students to not have to decode words. Instead, it allows them to focus on reading comprehension. Intervention time is not meant for a teacher to give independent work nor to just provide observation without support.

2. B: Word analysis and fluency should be mastered before teaching theme, text evidence, and writing. For English Language Learners and struggling readers, word analysis and fluency are often difficult barriers, which is why comprehension skills are not initially mastered. Theme is often a complex and inferential skill, which is developed later on. Text evidence is pulling answers to comprehension questions directly from a text and cannot be accomplished until readers can fluently read and understand the text. Writing skills generally come after comprehension skills are underway.

3. C: Genre is a means of categorizing text by its structure and literary elements. Fiction and nonfiction are both genre categories. Plot is the sequence of events that make a story happen.

4. A: Scanning future portions of the text for information that helps resolve a question is an example of self-monitoring. Self-monitoring takes advantage of a natural ability of students to recognize when they understand the reading and when they do not. KWL charts are used to help guide students to identify what they already know about a given topic. Metacognitive skills are when learners think about thinking. Directed reading-thinking activities are done before and after reading to improve critical thinking and reading comprehension.

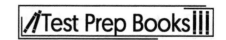

5. C: Comprehension is the level of content understanding that a student demonstrates after reading. Orthographic development is a cumulative process for learning to read, with each skill building on the previously mastered skill. Fluency is an automatic recognition and accurate interpretation of text. Phonics is the ability to apply letter-sound relationships and letter patterns in order to accurately pronounce written words.

6. A: Voice is the primary trait that shows the individual writing style of an author. It is based on an author's choice of common syntax, diction, punctuation, character development, dialogue, etc.

7. B: The key word here is "inform," which is the primary purpose of all informative modes. They contain facts, definitions, instructions, and other elements with the objective purpose of informing a reader—such as study guides, instruction manuals, and textbooks. Choice *A* is incorrect because an argumentative mode contains language that is subjective and is intended to persuade or to inform with a persuasive bias. Choice *C* is incorrect as a narrative mode is used primarily to tell a story and has no intention of informing, nor is the language inherently objective. Choice *D* is incorrect as descriptive modes possess no inherent intent to inform, and are used primarily to describe.

8. A: Editorials, recommendation letters, and cover letters all seek to persuade a reader to agree with the author, which reflects an argumentative mode. Choice *B* is incorrect because the intent of the examples is to persuade a reader to agree with the author, not to present information. Choice *C* is incorrect as editorials, letters of recommendation, and cover letters are not trying to tell a story. Choice *D* is also incorrect because while the examples may contain many descriptions, that is not their primary purpose.

9. B: Both the audience and primary purpose are important for choosing a writing mode. The audience is an important factor as the diction, tone, and stylistic choices of a written piece are tailored to fit the audience demographic. The primary purpose is the reason for writing the piece, so the mode of writing must be tailored to the most effective delivery method for the message. The main idea is the central theme or topic of the piece, which can be expressed in any form the author chooses. Because the mode depends on the reason the author wrote the piece, the main idea is not an important factor in determining which mode of writing to use.

10. C: The main idea of a piece is its central theme or subject and what the author wants readers to know or understand after they read. Choice *A* is incorrect because the primary purpose is the reason that a piece was written, and while the main idea is an important part of the primary purpose, the above elements are not developed with that intent. Choice *B* is incorrect because while the plot refers to the events that occur in a narrative, organization, tone, and supporting details are not used only to develop plot. Choice *D* is incorrect because characterization is the description of a person.

11. A: The passage describes a situation and then explains the causes that led to it. Also, it utilizes cause and effect signal words, such as *causes, factors, so,* and *as a result.* Choice *B* is incorrect because a compare and contrast order considers the similarities and differences of two or more things. Choice *C* is incorrect because spatial order describes where things are located in relation to each other. Finally, Choice *D* is incorrect because time order describes when things occurred chronologically.

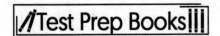

12. B: Children and less educated audiences tend to understand short, succinct sentences more effectively than longer, complex sentences because short sentences help increase information processing. Choice *A* is incorrect as longer, more fluid sentences are best used for adults and more educated audiences because they minimize processing times and allow for more information to be conveyed. Choices *C* and *D* are incorrect because there is no correlation between a given profession and a writing style; rather, it depends on how familiar the audience is with a given subject.

13. A: The revising stage involves adding, removing, and rearranging sections of a written work. Choice *B* is incorrect as the publishing stage involves the distribution of the finished product to the publisher, teacher, or reader. Choice *C* is incorrect because the writing stage is the actual act of writing the work, and generally does not including editing or revision. Choice *D* is incorrect as the pre-writing stage involves the planning, drafting, and researching of the intended piece.

Dear RICA Test Taker,

We would like to start by thanking you for purchasing this practice test book for your RICA exam. We hope that we exceeded your expectations.

We strive to make our practice questions as similar as possible to what you will encounter on test day. With that being said, if you found something that you feel was not up to your standards, please send us an email and let us know.

We would also like to let you know about other books in our catalog that may interest you.

RICA Study Guide

This can be found on Amazon: amazon.com/dp/1628454466

We have study guides in a wide variety of fields. If the one you are looking for isn't listed above, then try searching for it on Amazon or send us an email.

Thanks Again and Happy Testing!
Product Development Team
info@studyguideteam.com

Interested in buying more than 10 copies of our product? Contact us about bulk discounts:

bulkorders@studyguideteam.com

FREE Test Taking Tips DVD Offer

To help us better serve you, we have developed a Test Taking Tips DVD that we would like to give you for FREE. **This DVD covers world-class test taking tips that you can use to be even more successful when you are taking your test.**

All that we ask is that you email us your feedback about your study guide. Please let us know what you thought about it – whether that is good, bad or indifferent.

To get your **FREE Test Taking Tips DVD**, email freedvd@studyguideteam.com with "FREE DVD" in the subject line and the following information in the body of the email:

a. The title of your study guide.

b. Your product rating on a scale of 1-5, with 5 being the highest rating.

c. Your feedback about the study guide. What did you think of it?

d. Your full name and shipping address to send your free DVD.

If you have any questions or concerns, please don't hesitate to contact us at freedvd@studyguideteam.com.

Thanks again!

CPSIA information can be obtained
at www.ICGtesting.com
Printed in the USA
LVHW021236150623
749660LV00015B/1509